Love Is...

Love Is...

GRACE MAKOTO TAM

with John Tam & Tamami Okauchi

TATE PUBLISHING & *Enterprises*

Published by Tate Publishing & Enterprises, LLC
127 E. Trade Center Terrace | Mustang, Oklahoma 73064 USA
1.888.361.9473 | www.tatepublishing.com

Tate Publishing is committed to excellence in the publishing industry. The company reflects the philosophy established by the founders, based on Psalm 68:11,
"The Lord gave the word and great was the company of those who published it."

Published in the United States of America

ISBN: 978-1-61346-043-6
Biography & Autobiography / General
11.11.08

This book is lovingly dedicated in memory of our angel, Grace Makoto Tam.

ACKNOWLEDGEMENTS

Our sincere appreciation goes to teachers, friends, and families from Kellogg Marsh Elementary School and to our neighbors for their support of our family.

We also send thank you to those who have filled Grace's life with joy, love, and dreams.

TABLE OF CONTENTS

INTRODUCTION

One cold night in January 1999, she came to us. She was a quiet baby, as if she was content where she was.

We named her Grace, truly believing that God blessed us by giving her to us. Since then our life had been filled with love, laughter, and joy.

On July 31 in 2010, our family outing began at about eleven o'clock to the ice caves at Verlot. We arrived about eleven forty. We reached the top at about twelve thirty and took a lunch break— peanut butter and jam for myself; rice ball and various meat (salami and jerky) for others.

We reached the second caves at about one forty. After a photo was taken, we stood on the hill with an ice archway behind us. We were not inside the caves; we were standing about fifteen to seventeen feet in front of the cave. I was farther forward trying to take a picture for them. I heard a snapping sound, and the ice broke loose and came sliding down on the ground then rolled forward, bounced over Grace, and landed in front of her, not on top of her. The chunk of ice hit Grace at about two o'clock. Fellow hikers helped carry her down and rested her on a flat surface. Three of the people helping us were nurses. At first glance it looked like she only broke her left leg.

I told Gracie I love her and to please hang on, for help is on the way. She gripped very tight to my arm and told me she loves me too. We kept her warm with several donated jackets, shirts, etc. We kept talking to her to keep her awake. She said she was not in pain but just could not feel her legs.

We asked her questions, such as:

"What's your favorite food?"

She answered, "Pasta."

"Who's your favorite teacher?"

She answered, "Mr. Daoust."

"Who's your best friend?"

She answered, "Carrie."

"What's her last name?"

She answered, "Cha Cha Cha." (Actually her last name is Cha; Grace had a sense of humor.)

"What's your favorite fruit?"

She answered, "Mango, but it gives me a rash."

"Who's your favorite singer?"

She answered, "Taylor Swift."

"What's your favorite TV show?"

She answered, "Hannah Montana."

This went on for about one hour. The only complaint was that she felt dehydrated, so we gave her little bits of water. We kept her head from moving around with a rock on each side and her head resting on a couple of sweatshirts.

After one hour, one of the nurses said she could not find her pulse, so they started CPR. Her eyes were dilated. They did this for fifty minutes. They also tried to put oxygen into her with a drinking tube from my wife's drinking bottle.

The first help finally came, just a park ranger with nothing except a radio. Then shortly after, an emergency medical team came. The volunteers kept asking if they had suction, but they did not. The third help arrived at about four fifteen. They had a defibrillator. They tried to give Grace a couple shock treatments, and they soon failed, for the battery was gone after maybe two or three times. The person that operated the machine did not know how to change the battery, so another person had to help him. When they finally changed the battery, they found out the backup battery was not charged.

Overall we had waited nearly two and a half hours for help, but even life-sustaining effort didn't help her, and she passed away.

"I'm going to sleep," were her last words, and she went back to be with God quietly.

Grace made us feel special just because we were her parents. We miss her so much.

Inspiration of publishing this book came from the writing journal Grace kept writing throughout fifth grade. The fifth graders learned the various style of writing. Grace followed the instruction and wrote her own version.

Some are poems; some are short essay; some are fiction. Unfortunately one of her fantasy stories "The Mystery of the Island" is not finished. You can use your own imagination and finish the story for her.

This book also includes her travel journal, especially assigned by her teacher, when she was away from school to Hawaii, Japan, and Hong Kong.

We also thought of collecting the memories of Grace's friends, teachers, and neighbors. You will find the writings from the people Grace has spent time with during her short life on the earth.

In honor to Grace's dream, opening a shelter for less-fortunate dogs, all profits from sales of this book will be donated to the local animal shelters in Seattle, Washington, area.

Grace Makoto Tam Memorial Fund is established with Bank of America; a website dedicated to Grace is:

http://pnwhikes.com/grace/.

THINGS I LIKE

1. Sleepover
2. Mac & Cheese
3. Spaghetti
4. Birthday
5. Dancing with Mrs. Bierer
6. Ice cream sundae
7. Drawing and coloring
8. Presents for me
9. Rice with sauce
10. Japan
11. Gummy bears
12. Trips and traveling
13. Dogs and puppies
14. My dog, Sugar
15. My friends
16. Camping with my cousins of Spokane

THINGS I DON'T LIKE

1. Brussels sprouts
2. People making fun of me
3. Bossy people
4. My brother bothering me and my friends
5. Getting hurt

THINGS I WOULD LIKE TO DO

1. Save dogs
2. Travel to Paris and Italy
3. Own a huge house with an indoor pool
4. Make a volcano

A Letter from Savannah Pearson

I met Grace in third grade. Grace and Lyda were friends before I even knew Grace. It was my first year at Kellogg Marsh and I had no friends except Tana Wolfson. Lyda helped me to figure out where we were supposed to hang our coats and backpacks. Then that first recess I got another friend added to my list. Lyda introduced Grace to me, and I knew at first glance that Grace and I were destined to be friends.

From then on we played at recess together and I tried to sit by her as much as possible. I did this because she made me feel welcomed and accepted. She was always nice and anything that came out of her mouth was always uplifting and positive.

When she came over the first time, my entire family immediately loved her. She was kind and considerate. She was good at almost everything. She would laugh at Caleb's jokes even though they weren't funny. She did that just to humor him. If we had to sum Grace up in one word, we couldn't, because we couldn't describe her in just one way. It would take millions of words to do that. Everyone probably has a different word.

I remember the first time Grace came over for a sleepover and we had fish for dinner. My dad made something different for us to eat because we don't like fish. Dad assumed that Grace didn't either so he made chicken for the kids and fish for the adults. Well there was going to be some extra fish so my dad jokingly asked us if we wanted some fish and Grace piped up and said, "I do." My dad sort of looked at her and said okay and gave her some. Turns out she liked fish.

Well that night we stayed up late and I was ready to crash. So as soon as I got into bed I was asleep. Well Grace on the other hand didn't go straight to sleep. In fact, she couldn't sleep. She tried to wake me up a couple of times but I wouldn't budge so eventually she went down and got my dad and told him she couldn't sleep and so he went upstairs and woke me up and said, "Savannah, your friend can't sleep. Why don't you stay awake with her until she gets tired and then you both can sleep?" Well as soon as he left, I was asleep again and they couldn't wake me up.

Grace was a big fan of dogs and when she would come over she always loved on our dog,

Sophie. Last Wednesday Sophie got very sick and we had to put her down. We know Sophie is being well taken care of because Grace is with her.

Grace was an amazing friend. She always made me feel good. I will never forget her or the acceptance she gave me. She will forever be in my heart.

By Savannah Pearson
Friend

I LOVE YOU, MOM ...

I am thankful to have an extraordinary mom like my mom because... she is fun, caring, nice, loving, and helpful. There are so many things nice about my mom I can't list them all.

My mom is fun because she takes me to fun places like she took my brother and me to the zoo and we ate yummy lunch there. She is also fun because she took me to Japan and we went to luscious restaurant.

My mom is caring. When it was my birthday she got me exactly what I wanted, and surprised me. She is also caring because when I was crying she bolted outside and took me inside then she took me to the doctor's right away and comforted me. She is caring because when I couldn't sleep or I had nightmares my mom would come and sleep with me and I would feel much better. My mom is caring, even though she doesn't feel well she still has a smile on her face and takes care of us, no matter what. If she is busy or tired she will still take care of us. My mom is caring because when I went to a sleepover I said I wanted to go home, so my mom bolted to the house and picked me up.

My mom is nice because she tucks my brother and me in bed. She is also nice because she makes my favorite dishes like pasta and curry.

My mom is loving because she kisses me every night and gives me hugs every night. She is also loving because she makes sure I get three kisses every night and my night-light is on. She is loving cause I say everything I need to say and she listens to every word I say and she makes sure I go to sleep. She is also loving because when I had a bad day she comforted me and made me feel much better.

My mom is helpful because when I go to birthday parties or sleepovers she drives me there. She is also helpful. She helps me with my homework and when I need to my flashcards.

I am thankful to have an extraordinary mom like my mom because... she is fun, caring, nice, loving, and helpful. My mom is like the cloud to drift me away and the sun to brighten my day.

Love,
Your Daughter,
Grace
Mother's Day 2009

A Letter from Mom

Dear Grace:

Mom had no idea that good-bye comes so suddenly. Mom still remembers the day you were born. You came to us 10 days earlier than due day. Mom and Daddy had no idea what was going to happen next, and we just drove the car as fast as possible to the hospital. When I held you in my arms for the first time, I felt like this was the best thing that had happened in my life.

Do you remember you and I were planning to try out Facebook together during the summer break? We also planned I live close to you and do baby sit of your children when you get married and have children. I didn't tell you, but Mom was dreaming herself of maneuvering the ups and downs of the life with teenage Grace, and also of choosing your wedding gown together. None of them come true in this world. Mom, however, hasn't given up. I will see you sometime in heaven and my dreams come true at that time.

Your 12th birthday came on January 14th, 2011. William, Sugar, Dad, and Mom celebrated your birthday with your favorite meal, "pasta." Guess what you got for a birthday present from the neighbors? It is a beautiful bench at our detention pond facing an island and a small path. It has a plate with your name on, saying you were a "beautiful daughter and sister, and wonderful friend." At the night of 14th, Jamie and Kristen, Caden and Chloe, and Austyn and Kameryn walked with us to the bench. They took turns to sit there. Mom could see you sitting among them with a smile on your face. Your friends from the neighborhood remember you and the bench always brings fun memories to them.

One thing good happened after your death is we met a whole lot of people who is willing to support us. Your teachers from Kellogg Marsh were incredibly supportive to think about William's well-being. Your friends and their parents were compassionate to visit to see us with beautiful flowers. Your neighbors were generously kind to make sure we are not alone and to knock on the door with warm meals and hugs and tears. We also met other parents who lost their child too soon. They know Mom and Daddy's pain, agony, and emptiness. They just comfort our soul by listening to our stories.

Grace, you are so caring that you delivered get-well-cards to me every night when I was really sick.

Grace, you are so sweet that you always gave in when there was an argument.

Grace, you are so determined that you finished your 5th grade project by yourself.

Grace, you are so kind that you took good care of Sugar who used to be a stray dog.

Grace, you are so considerate that you cried and worried when you saw a little girl selling candies in Mexico.

Grace, you are so smart that you dream of the future people won't depend of oil.

Grace, you are so loving that you brought to Dad and Mom such a joy and pride to be your parents.

On July 31st we had lunch together and I asked you, "Is lunch good?" Instead of saying yes, you just pointed your thumb up and showed a big smile. That was the last smile I saw. Mom misses you so much and loves you forever. Thank you so much for being my daughter. I am thinking of you every day.

Mom

MY BOO BOO

When I was camping, I went down to the beach and I was jumping on rocks. Then I came to our campsite and all of a sudden I screamed and my mom was wondering what happened and my toe was all red and puffed up. After a couple of days it was so itchy! I hated it. I am scared to go down to the beach now.

September 14, 2009

DON'T TAKE THINGS FOR GRANTED

Because if you look at your life and the boy's life, he has a very poor life. You should be thankful that you can go to school and learn. Look at what you have, be thankful what you have. Be thankful for your house and bed. Don't just brag about your stuff. Also be thankful for food and your home.

DO I HAVE A NICKNAME?

My nickname from my dad is Gracie.

But it makes me feel embarrassed.

From my mom and my brother I don't have a nickname.

I don't know why I don't have a nickname from my mom and my brother.

My grandpa and my grandma and almost all my relatives call me Gracie.

September 14, 2009

A Letter from Lyda Ebadani

I met Grace when I was two years old in the Marysville library.

Throughout the years, I got to know Grace better. In third grade, we were in the same class. A year later, I moved to a different school, but we still kept in touch a lot. She would come over. I would go over. And it went on. We had very fun time together.

The last time I saw Grace was five to six days before the accident. She was at my house for a sleepover. I remember that day we played slip and slide and water gun with neighbors and we laughed a lot. She was very kind, nice, funny, and very friendly, never mean to me.

We had very fun memories and sleep-overs and birthday parties. It was fun time just being with her and around her.

You will be missed.

Your BFF,
Lyda Ebadani
Friend

DANCING WITH MRS. BIERER

Has Your Class Ever Danced on Stage Together?

Last year me and my whole class did dancing, and we did a dance called Cupid Shuffle. We practiced it for like half of the year. We did some more dances like Rainy Night and Electric Slide. It was so fun dancing with Mrs. Bierer.

Finally the talent show came, and we danced on the stage. It was a blast!

I wish I could do it again, but I couldn't. I really miss Mrs. Bierer. I wish I could repeat that year over dancing with Mrs. Bierer.

September 22, 2009

A Poem from Mrs. Bierer

When tomorrow starts without
me, and I'm not there to see,
The sun will rise and find your eyes
all filled with tears for me,
I wish so much you wouldn't cry
the way you did today,
While thinking of the many
things, we didn't get to say.

I know how much you love me,
as much as I love you,
And each time that you think of
me, I know you'll miss me too,
Life at times will catch you unawares
but please try to understand,
That an angel came and called my
name, and took me by the hand.

He said my place was ready, in
heaven way up above,
And that I'd have to leave behind
all those I dearly loved.
As I turned to walk away, the
tears fell from my eyes,
For all my life I'd always thought
I didn't want to die.

I had so much to live for, so much left yet to do,
It seemed so very cruel to me
that I was leaving you.
Thoughts of all our yesterdays,
the good ones and the bad,
Are remembered for all the love we
shared especially the fun we had.

If I could relive just yesterday,
even for a short while,
I'd say my goodbyes and kiss you,
and hopefully see you smile.
As the days pass into weeks,
don't think we're far apart,
For every time you think of me,
I'll be there in your heart.

Alisha Bierer
Fourth grade teacher

COLORING AND DRAWING

I love to color and draw. This summer I took a drawing class. I am not really good at drawing compare to the other people. Even though I am not so good I still did learn to draw and color really well. This summer I really improved on my drawing.

September 23, 2009

A Letter from Jenny and Olivia Brice

Grace was always friendly and playful and was my buddy in preschool. We liked to play dress-up and blocks. She was always ready to do more activities again and again. She made me feel happy and will always be a warm memory for me.

Olivia Brice, age 11

I remember Grace as a happy little girl who explored her world with curiosity and great imagination. Her art contribution to the preschool quilt we purchased at the auction in 2002 has more variety of color than any of the other 36 squares. To me, this is a beautiful metaphor for the rainbow of color she brought to the lives of those who knew and loved her.

Jenny Brice, Olivia's mother

MY DOG SUGAR

I love my dog Sugar a lot.

I was very bored in the summer, so Sugar usually took naps with me and played with me. Every morning me and my brother go out to take her on a walk. Sometimes I dress my dog as a bride or fairy. When I grow up, I want to take care of dogs and own a shelter.

Whenever I am with Sugar, I always feel happy. Without my dog Sugar I feel lonely and bored. Whenever I need to read, I set out a blanket and pillows for me and Sugar to lay down on. Then I start reading and Sugar sleeps right next to me. Sugar gets a million kisses a day. I am glad I have Sugar as company.

September 23, 2009

A Letter from Minako Takahashi

Grace was an unusually loving and responsible girl for eleven years old. She intensively loved people and dogs as if she knew she did not have much time left to share her love and care with us. She wanted to do everything more than at her best and please us. She never reserved her love and care for anybody.

Grace shocked me when I picked up my dog, Sophie, at Grace's house after two weeks of her first dog-sitting Sophie. Grace crying and chasing after Sophie seen in my car rear window will stay in my mind forever. I felt so guilty to take my dog away from that gentle and loving girl. She was looking forward to taking care of Sophie again once she learned that Sophie would come back. I felt so comfortable and safe to leave my dog, a five pounds dachshund to Grace. Sophie loved to jump on Grace's laps and licked her face endlessly.

Grace was a super special girl for dogs. Grace was so excited when Sugar, her new lovable dog, came into her life. She and her brother, William, gave Sugar rains of hugs and kisses to Sugar as soon as they returned home from school. They could not wait to see Sugar. Sugar loved it! Sugar knew that she finally found somebody who really loved and cared for her. Grace took care of Sugar and Sophie as if she were their responsible mom. They trusted Grace.

Sugar and Sophie are extremely lucky dogs who received Grace's intensive and special love and sweetness. They miss Grace as much as we all who know her do. Now they know it is time for them to give Grace's love to dogs at where Grace has gone. I can see that Grace is busy for looking after many dogs there.

Thank you very much, Grace, for all of your generous love.

Minako Takahashi
Friend

DID SOME MORE DANCES

My class did some more dances. The first one is Rainy Night (one of my favorites). It's where you go backward on your feet and also go forward. You start stepping forward.

Cupid Shuffle is the one which we did it at the talent show. You first shuffle to the right; then you shuffle to the left. After that you kick up your heel, and you do it around in circle till the music is over (one of my favorites).

Electric Slide is you step out, step behind, and then step out and then together. Then you do it on the other side. And you keep dancing it in a circle till the music stops.

September 28, 2009

A LETTER FROM EMMA ARTZ

Hi, my name is Emma Artz. It was the beginning of my fourth grade year and I met a very special person, Grace. It was 9:00 A.M. when we arrived at Grace's bus stop. Grace was kind of shy, so I offered her to sit with me. I said hi, she also said hi in a caring, soft voice. We instantly became friends.

Five months later, it was Grace's birthday. She invited me. It was a slumber party! We played hide and seek. I was on Grace's team. After that we all had cake. It was delicious! Grace's party was amazing!

Three months later, it was my birthday. I invited Grace. I also had a slumber party. We did so many fun things together! My mom, sister, and my mom's friend helped us out with my party. We did makeup, painted our nails, sang karaoke, and ate pizza!

At school, Grace and I played with each other at recess; we always ran up to the swings before anyone else would take them! Grace was also smart. She always helped me with my math. We both loved puppies; also she liked to draw just like me. We had so much in common!

I also remember when we went on a field trip to the Underground Tour of Seattle. She was in my group. My mom bought us ice-cream and we ate lunch by the pier.

I am a very lucky person to have had Grace in my life. We had lots of cherishing moments together. My birthday is in two weeks and I know Grace will be there with me.

Emma Artz
Friend

BACTERIA

"The Good, The Bad, and The Stinky"

by Joy Masoff

There are good and bad bacteria. For example, if you eat at McDonald's, maybe, the cook didn't wash his hands after the bathroom, and then you get the bad bacteria, if you eat the food. Bacteria can spread into so many pieces. Ten thousand bacteria is only an inch long. So be careful of what you do because there are many bad bacteria in the world.

November 13, 2009

A Letter from
Isaiah Cummins

Grace was so special to us. Every time we saw her we filled with joy and happiness. We were always friends and hardly got into fights. As we remember Grace, we will cherish our memories with her. I will remember Grace as a kind, caring, honest, and funny. As we think of Grace, we think of sadness and happiness. Throughout all the years I knew Grace, she was shy and quiet, but when she was with her friends, she would fill with joy. She would run all over the playground and play with Carrie and me. Usually if I had no one to play with I would go talk with Carrie and Grace. In Mr. Daoust's class we would make fun of him all the time. We even made a newspaper about him! The last time I saw Grace was at Relay for Life at Asbury field, and she was with her friend Meghan Sparr, and I only saw her once or twice and she was just walking around.

I wish I could have seen her the last time and get to say good-bye to her. She was such a good friend. I was devastated when I found out that Grace had died. I had cried myself to sleep for days when I thought about her.

The hardest part was to see her body at the viewing. I was going to cry but I don't like crying in front of people.

All I hope is that Tamami and John are doing all right.

Thank you, Tamami and John, for letting me write something for the book. I am honored.

Isaiah Cummins
Friend

"FLY AWAY HOME"

by Eve Bunting

In *Fly Away Home* by Eve Bunting, the boy Andrew and his father live in an airport.

They always are wearing blue coats not to get noticed.

The boy really wants to be free. When the blue bird got out, he felt like he was free.

The boy and Dad share their money with Danny. The boy tries to save as much money as possible in his shoe.

Eve Bunting says to me, "Don't take things for granted."

November 18, 2009

A LETTER FROM NATALIE GRIMM

In second grade Grace and I were in the same class and our teacher was Mrs. Beason. Grace loved reading; her favorite author was Eve Bunting. Eve Bunting wrote many books, but the one I remember most is *Fly Away Home*. *Fly Away Home* is about a kid who lives in an airport with his dad. The boy and the dad wore all blue so they wouldn't get noticed. Every day they switched airline terminals to sleep in. One day a bird flew into their terminal and couldn't find its way out. So it sat on the ledge and finally after a while it got out. The bird influenced the boy to save money in his shoe so he and his dad could get an apartment. We talked about appreciating our lives and being thankful for even little things.

Grace was one of the nicest people I've ever known. If someone was out on the playground alone, I remember that Grace would go over to them and ask them to play with her. Grace was so kind-hearted and made sure to include kids.

Grace was also very talented. We did a lot of crafts in second grade and all the ones she did turned out so amazing. My favorite memory of Grace is when she came to my house on my birthday. We went to the beach and had so much fun building sand castles and flipping over rocks at the beach. We were looking for tiny baby crabs and when we saw them we giggled so much! The tiny crabs tickled our hand when we picked them up. We put them in a bucket and later we let them go. Grace told me that she loved the beach so much!

I will never forget Grace. I miss Grace and the happiness in her heart. Someday I think Grace and I will play together on the beaches in Heaven.

Natalie Grimm
Friend

HAWAII TRIP

12–1-2009

Today I had to go on the plane for 5 and a half hours. I got a huge headache, and I felt very sick. I played my DS, and I took a nap right before the plane landed. Then finally the plane landed. I was very excited. I hopped out of the plane, and we waited for our luggage. Then a yellow bus picked us up so we could go to the place where rent a car. Finally we got to go grocery shopping, then go to our time-share. My mom said we could go in the pool. The pool was sort of cold, but if you get used to it, it is warm. Then it was dinner time, and after dinner we went for a walk to the beach. I took beautiful scenery pictures. Then we went back for a swim. Finally it was time to be done for the day.

12–2-2009

Today I had to go to a breakfast meeting. It is a breakfast where you can book other places like going on a submarine or a hula dance. My mom and dad booked the submarine which we are going on tomorrow. We had pastries and fruits (fresh pineapple). Then me, my brother, and my dad went up to our room, and we changed into our bathing suits. Then me and my brother jumped in the pool, and I did flips in the water. After my mom and dad were done with the meeting, they said for us to come down to the room because we were going to farmers' market. I didn't buy anything at farmers' market because I was comparing prices. Then we walked back to our time-share. It was very hot and tiring. Finally we got back and had lunch. After lunch we went in the swimming pool for 2 hours. Then we drove to a beach and took pictures with turtles. After that we went to a Japanese restaurant. I got very sick and had a huge headache. So after dinner we drove to our time-share, and I went to bed right away.

12–3–2009 Submarine!

Today we got to sleep in and for breakfast, we had pancakes, sausage, and fresh mango. (Yesterday we went mango picking.) Today in the morning I had a huge headache. My mom and my brother went swimming while I sat on a sun chair. After half an hour, we went back for cooking lunch. We had pizza and pineapples. Then we started driving to the submarine place. A big boat took us to the submarine. I took a seat and watched where we were headed. Finally we arrived at the submarine. I climbed down the ladder into the submarine. It was pretty dark in there. In a couple of minutes we started to move. I saw a lot of fish. We saw lots of yellow fish. There were lots of shipwrecks. The deepest we went was 109 feet down the water. The ride was over. We came back and started walking to other stores. Then we went into the hot, hot car. After we arrived at the time-share, I went swimming in the pool. After an hour we ate dinner outside by the pool. We had barbecued pork and rice, and also vegetables. Finally after an hour I went to relax in the hot tub with my family. Then it was bedtime for all of us.

12–4–2009 Akaka Falls!

Today I had waken up early because we were going to a lot of places. But when we got outside, it was raining cats and dogs. Still we decided to drive to Hilo. Hilo is on the other side of Hawaii. We drove an hour and a half. We stopped to pick sugar cane! I picked sugar cane out of the real plant. I got to taste sugar canes! Fresh! Then we drove to the biggest water fall in Hawaii. It was very big. I saw lots of unusual plants. Then we drove another hour or so, I don't really know, to the black sand beach. It actually has black sand. We saw quite a few turtles. Me and my brother collected black sand. My dad got a coconut from the ground. Then we went back to the car and drove to a coconut tree. My dad lifted my mom, and she knocked down a coconut. Then we drove to a bakery and bought some donuts. Finally we drove to our time-share. We were out for 9 and half hours. We were driving for about 7 and half hours! I was exhausted when we got back. We cut the 2 coconuts and ate some of them. I don't like the milk though. Finally we had dinner and me, my mom and my brother played Old Maid, Gold Fish, and Crazy Eights. Finally everyone went to bed.

12–5–2009 *Hula Dance*

Today in the morning my brother drove me crazy. He woke me up too early for me. We had cereal and eggs for breakfast. Then we went down to the pool. I was playing with another boy, who is from Olympia. We were playing catch the ball. Then I went up for lunch, and we had rice and chicken. Then we drove in our car for 40 minutes. Then we were at a shopping center to see a hula dance.

First we went shopping. Then me and my mom went to see the hula dance. There were two girls dancing, then there were little girls dancing. I took a picture with them. I got to learn and dance with them on the stage. Other people got to, too. Then my family and me ate some dinner. I got noodles. Then we got ice cream. I got birthday cake flavor. Then we drove to our time-share. Then I took a shower and went to bed.

12–6-2009 *Snorkeling*

Today I was not feeling well in the morning because last night I didn't sleep well. We had cinnamon pancakes for breakfast. My dad was upset. Then we went to the farmers' market, before we were about to leave, my mom and dad got mad at each other. Then we started walking to the farmer's market. I bought a purple shiny turtle necklace. I also bought an anklet. My mom and dad bought a welcome sign for our house. Then we walked to the ABC store. We bought drinks. I bought Mountain Dew. Then we stopped by the beach for taking a break, after that we headed back to our time-share. We had lunch, then we got ready to go to the beach. I went snorkeling with my mom. I saw so many fish and they are colorful. I was in the ocean! Then we went back to the time share. I took a shower. Then I relaxed for a while. Then we had dinner and we went by the pool and play card games. I won 2 out of 3 times. Then I watched TV and went to bed.

12–7-2009 *The Last Full Day*

Today I had cereal for breakfast. It was the last full day. After breakfast we went snorkeling again, because I wanted to go again. So we went again. I saw lots of fish and turtles. It looked like the turtle was waving at me. Then we drove back to our time-share. Me and my brother went in the hot tub because we were cold. My mom came down and played with us. We had popcorn for a snack. After that we went up for lunch. We had top ramen, one of my favorites! After lunch we settled down, then me and my brother went swimming. I did a jumping jack jump. My mom took pictures of me and my brother. Then we went back to our room and watched TV for half an hour. At 5:30 pm we watched the sunset. It was beautiful! Then we ate dinner. We had leftovers. After that we settled down, then we went swimming again. After swimming we took a shower and went to bed.

Hawaii 83 degrees. Seattle Low 14 degrees.

MORE LUNCH CHOICES

I think all schools should have more lunch choices. I have three reasons for this idea. First, more students will buy lunch. Second, it is good for kids to have a variety so kids can stay healthy and stay in shape. Third, there will be less waste because kids actually eat the foods.

If more students buy lunch that means you will make more money. The company will have a profit. The kids will probably buy the lunch because there are more lunch choices. For example some kids don't like the sloppy joe and the mac and cheese, but if we have more lunch choices, more kids will like to buy lunch and maybe pay more because the kids like the foods.

Lots of kids aren't healthy because there is not a variety of lunch choices. Kids will be healthy and not get stomachaches because they have a variety of choices. Parents will be happy because their kids are healthy and staying in shape. For example, my parents don't like me buying lunch because they think I won't be healthy and there is not a good variety of lunch choices.

Lots of kids throw away their food and that is a very bad waste. Wasting food is the wasting money, but if we have more lunch choices less kids will waste food and you will not be wasting money. For example, when I throw away my garbage, I see lots of food being thrown in the garbage and that is a total waste of money.

JAPAN

I was getting on the plane and I was so excited to go to Japan. We had to say good bye to my dad. Finally on the plane we had snacks and drinks. I played my DS and we watched movies. I slept for an hour. It was a short plane ride, 2 hours. Then we got onto our second plane which was 10 hours long! Finally we were at Japan!

I was so excited. We met my grandpa and grandma at the airport. We got in my aunt's car and we drove to my grandma and grandpa's house. It was a two-hour ride. My aunt's house is right across from their house. It's so close. You just walk two steps and then you are there! I was so excited to see their house again.

In about two hours later my cousin came home from school! We played our DS together. A couple days later we went to the zoo. In Japan we went to places like the fair, Nara (ancient capital of Japan), my mom's old work, lots of parks, and the aquarium.

When we were in Nara, I got a lucky charm. It's for good luck. You can make a wish on it, then it might come true.

Finally it was time for me to go home. I was very sad. I cried all the way home. And when we got home, Sugar was so excited to see us. But I kept crying. I can't wait till I get to go to Japan again!

A LETTER FROM COUSIN AYUMU

You are Dan-chan's daughter. You know, Dan-chan is a nickname of your mother which I named.

I liked Dan-chan very much when I was a child because she took good care of me.

I wanted to take care of you like Dan-chan did.

When your family came to Japan, we played a lot; DS, card games, drawing pictures, etc.

I remember you were always laughing. You looked like very fun and I was happy.

Especially, you laughed so much when William, Hikaru and I were fighting against each other.

You and William woke me up every day. It was really hard for me. I am not still good at getting up early in the morning.

I heard that you passed away before my entrance examination for graduate school. I was so sad.

I was going to see you with Hikaru after the examination to please you.

I know you were anxious for us to visit your house. I regret that I could not go to America. I'm sorry.

I took the examination with your hair and funny picture which you drew for me.

I passed the examination in your favor.

I pray to you before important event. You always help me. Thank you very much.

I thought that you will live in Japan someday.

You were a very kind girl. I wanted you to teach me English in the future.

And I wanted to teach Japanese for you.

I believe that you sometimes visit my house.

I'm going to live in the apartment by myself in coming spring. I want you to wake me up at seven.

Finally, please watch over your family in America, Hong Kong and Japan forever.

Cousin Ayumu

TRIP TO JAPAN AND HONG KONG

Japan 5–2-2010 to 5–3-2010

Today was one of the worst days. I had to say good-bye to our dog, Sugar. She was very sad. We rode on a shuttle to the airport. Then we found our airline, Asiana. The airplane ride was 11 hours long. I did some math, then I watched *Alvin and the Chipmunks, the Squeakquel.* It was hilarious. They served us dinner, but I wasn't hungry. I tried to fall asleep, but the airplane was too loud. Since I couldn't sleep, I watched *The Spy Next Door.* It was also hilarious! I also watched some of *New Moon.* Finally I got so exhausted, I went to sleep. When I woke up on the plane, I felt so exhausted, and my ears were plugged up. We arrived at Korea. I took a look around. My head hurt. Then we went on our 1 hour and 45 minutes plane ride. I wasn't feeling well at all. So I went to the bathroom. When I got back, I threw up. It was horrifying. We finally arrived at Osaka, Japan. We got our luggage and met my mom's family there.

They were late to pick us up, because of the traffic jam. The plane ride had really good service, but I hated it. I hate airplanes. When we got back to my grandma's house, I said hi to everyone. Then I took a bath. The bath you take is a combination of a shower and bath. I like it. Then I was so exhausted and I went to bed.

Japan 5–4–2010

Today I wake up 5:00 A.M. Japan time. I only got 3 hours of sleep. I was exhausted. I am still not used to the time change. We had sausage, toast, and Yakuruto drink. It was delicious. I like the really thick toast. After that it was 8:00 A.M., and my brother and me woke up my older cousin Ayumu. (His nickname is Ayu-chan.) He is really lazy. Then at 9:00 A.M. we woke up my younger cousin Hikaru. (His nick name is Hika-chan.) They are both lazy. Me and William were laughing. I have 2 cousins in Japan (Hikaru and Ayumu). They always wake up late and go to bed late. After that we and my family went to the park to watch my grandpa play games. Then we relaxed at home and my great aunt came over. She gave me and my brother 5000 yen ($50). We celebrated my brother's birthday. Before that we went to pick up the cake. We had rice with mushrooms and carrots and some other stuff. (I don't remember.) Then we sang the happy birthday song to my brother. He was happy. My cousins are so nice! Hikaru is 16 and Ayumu is 21 years old. Then we took my great aunt to the train station, and we walked to the beach. It was very hot outside. I was sweating like a pig. We walked back, and I had a huge headache. Then me and my cousins all played DS. We played Mario Kart DS. Me, William, and Hikaru all went against Ayumu. We did that many times. It made me feel better. At dinner, I felt like throwing up. I ate some udon noodle for dinner and felt a lot better. We took an evening walk to make me feel better. Then I took a bath and immediately fell asleep at 8:30 P.M. Japan time.

Japan 5–5-2010

Today I woke up at 7:00 A.M. We had thick toast and scrambled eggs. When I was done, me and my brother woke up my cousins again. They said, "Five more minutes." My brother really woke them up. After that I helped make rice balls for lunch. We are going to the Akashi Bridge. My family and my cousin's family went, not my grandma and grandpa. We had lunch and walked around. My aunt bought us takoyaki (made of flour and squid). The rice balls were delicious. Then we walked to the other side of the rest area and went inside. The place was famous for onions. They had lots of samples. Some were good. It was steaming hot outside. Then we came back into our car. Me and my brother played with my cousin in the car. We kept hitting each other with the balloon on the head. When we got back, we rested and I played cards with my grandma and my younger cousin. My cousin won most of the times. Then we had dinner. We went for sushi at a sushi restaurant. They serve us by making sushi go around on the conveyer, so you can reach and get it. It was delicious. I ate 5 plates. My brother ate 10 plates. If you collect 5 plates and play a game then you might get a prize, only if you are lucky. I got 3 prizes, so did my brother. I was lucky this time! Then we all went back and me and my brother and younger cousin played hide and seek. Hikaru was the best. Then my older cousin played cards and made a tower out of cards. We kept laughing, and it fell down. Then we took a bath and went to bed.

Japan 5–6-2010

Today I woke up at 7:30 A.M. We had Mister Donuts donuts for breakfast. They were delicious. Then my younger cousin went to school. Then later my older cousin went to school. Then me and my family went grocery shopping. You can walk! I really like Japan. When we got back my mom helped me make a map of all the parks around where my relatives live. After making a map, we had lunch. We had fish that we picked up at the grocery store. It was good, but there were lots of bones. Then we got ready and walked to the train station. We had to run to catch the train. My mom bought tickets to go on the train. The train was quite nice. Then we came to our stop, and we went shopping. I bought a couple of souvenirs. My mom bought fireworks for tonight. Then we stopped by the pet area. The dogs were adorable, but to me they looked sad to be in a cage. We went back, and I played cards with some of my relatives. I kept loosing. Then we had dinner. We had pancakes (but salty). They were so good. I had 2 and half pancakes. When my cousin came back, we used half of the fireworks. We saved another half for tomorrow night. Then we had a hot bath, and I went to bed. My grandma also said we could keep one of her stuffed animals. It is adorable.

Japan 5–7–2010

Today I woke up at 7:30 A.M. We had toast again. It was raining really hard outside. My younger cousin went to school. My older cousin stayed home until after lunch. My older cousin played with us. He was practicing for his presentation. He is a very good student. Only 3 students get picked. We were laughing a lot. My brother was being naughty. We had yakisoba noodle with vegetables. It was one of my favorites. Then he went to his presentation. My mom, grandma, and my aunt went to a massage place next door. I was going to go and watch, but my younger cousin came home. I decided to stay. First we played Mario Kart DS, but the game was not working. So we played Mario Party. My cousin won the first round, and my brother won the second round. I didn't win anything. Then we decided to play hide and seek. We got really sweaty and hot. So we went outside to play at the parks. We went to 4 or 5 different parks. At the last park we played at the most. We played on the teeter totter and did flips on the flipping bars. We also played with sand. Then we came back, and my older cousin was home. He said he did really good. Then we had dinner. You can make your own sushi. It was delicious. Then my cousins and me played Mario Party. We stopped to do fireworks. Then I took a bath and went to bed. I was crying, cause I didn't want to say good-bye.

Good-bye Japan, Hello Hong Kong
5–8–2010

Today I gave my relatives a hug and said good-bye. I was crying. I won't see them for 2 years. My uncle and aunt drove us to the airport. We ate rice balls and sausage for breakfast. After a while we said good-bye. I was crying. Then our plane took off. I was crying. The next plane was 3 and half hours, and the last plane was 2 hours and 40 minutes. We stopped in Beijing. My mom and dad bought a nice tea set, and it cost a lot. At the next plane, I threw up. I didn't feel well. I slept on the both planes. We finally arrived in Hong Kong. We took a taxi to our hotel. It is a very nice hotel. We are on the 15th floor. We are very high. Our view is very pretty. We settled down, and my grandma finally arrived. Two people brought her. She is very old. She was so happy to see us, but she can't speak English. One of the persons who brought her loves dogs, so do I. We all went out to eat together. I only ate rice soup and fish and vegetables. It was awesome. The two people left, and my Dad's sister came over. They went up to our room and talked. We have 2 rooms. One for my grandma and one for us. My grandma walks so slow. It takes like half an hour for her to walk. Then we went to bed. I was exhausted.

Facts about Japan

Temperature: 72–73 degrees (Spring Time)
Stayed at: Akashi-city

1. You can walk to many places like parks and even grocery stores.
2. The houses are so close.
3. Lots of apartments.
4. Have tatami floor instead of carpet.
5. Sleep in futon instead of bed.
6. Have shrines to protect the country.
7. Lots of rice fields and fresh sea food.
8. The car is very narrow and always drives on left side. The driver is on right side.
9. Lots of trains.
10. People always take off shoes when enter the house.
11. Yard is very small.
12. People don't have garages.

I really like Japan. You can walk to a lot of places which is nice. I really want to move there. But there is lots of seasonal allergies. The tatami floor is very nice. I also like the shutters. I like Japan a lot.

You subtract 4 from the time in Japan and switch A.M. and P.M. That is the time in Washington, USA at daylight saving time. For example. When it is 6 P.M. in Japan, it is 2 A.M. in Washington.

Hong Kong 5–9-2010

Today I woke up at 3:00 A.M. I am still not used to the time change. Me and my mom stayed up for a while. We got out of bed at 6:00 a,m. I was very tired. We ate at 9:30 A.M., because we had a table assigned. We ate dim sum, such as shrimp balls, sticky rice, rice soup, and barbecue buns. It was very good. I ate quite a lot. After breakfast we walked back to our room and went into the swimming pool. It was steaming hot outside. The purpose we are here is to visit my grandma. She took a while to walk there. I slid down the slide. It was cold at first, but once you get used, it is not so cold. Then me and my brother and my dad went down to the beach. The sand is as soft as flour. You can walk on bare feet. I also collected shells. When we got back, we went out for lunch. We went to McDonald's and got something for Grandma. My dad got a wheelchair for my grandma, so she can go around much faster. It was very hot. So we rested for a while. My grandma was quite tired. Then me and my family went to the dolphin statue park. When we came back we went for a walk and looked at souvenirs. Then we ate dinner outside. We had to. I was sweating so much. My dad bought us a drink. When we got back, I took a shower and went to bed.

Hong Kong 5–10–2010

Today I woke up at 7:00 A.M. We ate breakfast at the buffet in the hotel. It was sort of expensive, but really good. I ate a lot so I won't have lunch. When we were done, we went back to our room. It was a very stormy day, but it was very humid still. We went back and stayed and relaxed for a while. My brother had a fever and stayed in bed. And my family except for my brother went to check our email. Then we came back to my brother. We weren't going to have lunch, because we had a big breakfast. My brother woke up and we decided to take a walk to the park. There were lots of wedding decorations. When we arrived at the park, it started to rain, so we came back. On the way back we took pictures with the wedding decorations. Then me and my family went up stairs and played cards. I was winning almost all the way, but my mom got less points than me. My grandma kept watching us play. When we were done, we watched TV. We watched a Japanese show. Then went to the lobby to eat dinner. My aunt was coming over to stay the night and have dinner and breakfast with us. We ate noodles, fried rice, salad with rolls, and some chicken. It was awesome. After dinner was done, we went to the lobby and took good pictures. Then we went back to the hotel and had cake my aunt brought. Then we went to bed.

Hong Kong 5–11–2010

Today I woke up at about 7:30 am. My aunt and my grandma weren't awake yet. So me and my brother played Mario Kart on DS, while my mom and dad were working out in the exercise room. When my Aunt Lisa woke up, we took 2 taxis to a Chinese restaurant. We ate dim sum. It took a long time to get the food ready. My dad's brother came to visit. He ate brunch with us. When we were done, we all went shopping. My dad bought bakery and fruits. He also bought mochi. It was very good. Me and my brother both bought a pair of crocs for summer time. At the mall I bought a pair of shoes and my brother got new Legos. We kept walking around looking at stuff. My uncle went away and we said good-bye. My aunt also went away. After that we went back to our hotel and we went swimming. It was too cold. So we decided to go to the park again. This time it wasn't raining. It was very fun to play. Then we went out for dinner. We went to a noodle place. It was interesting, because we had it with macaroni. When we were finished we went back and went to bed.

Hong Kong 5–12–2010

Today we ate the bakery we bought yesterday. It was very good. We said good-bye to my grandma. I was sad. We checked out of the hotel. We got in a taxi and drove to the airport. Our first airplane was 3 hours long. I didn't puke! My second airplane was 9 hours and 15 minutes. I almost puked, because I ate. I watched the movie *Tooth Fairy*. It was hilarious. When we got to Seattle, we got our luggage and went through lots of stuff. Then we drove to my mom's friend's house and got our dog Sugar. She was so happy to see us.

When we got back home, I gave her a bath. She hated it. Then we ate dinner and went right to bed. I was exhausted.

Facts about Hong Kong

Temperature: 80–90 degree. Tropical climate.
Stayed at: Gold Coast Hotel at Tuen Moon

1. You can always swim.
2. The weather is steaming hot.
3. Lots of fresh fruits to eat.
4. Sometimes it can rain very hard.
5. Lots of palm trees.
6. Main seaport of South China.
7. A very very very small island.

I think Hong Kong is very hot, and it has very fresh fruits, but I wouldn't like the weather to be hot all the time. Very small and almost everyone lives in apartments.

MY AUNT'S HOUSE

My aunt's house is so close to my grandparents'
house.

I just take ten small steps and I'm there.

I like how it is so close to my aunt's house.

I don't even have to hop in the car.

I wish my house was next to their house.

Sometimes me and my brother go across their
house and pretend I live there and he lives there.

A Letter from Aunt Yukiyo

My sweet niece, Grace.

Your aunt's house is just next to your grandparents' house. You took only a few steps from Granma's door to my house, and opened the sliding door to come and visit us. I wish you lived next to me and came over every day. In the morning you said, "Good morning, Aunty," in Japanese. I still remember your bashful smile when you came in. One time I didn't understand you asking, "Can I use a computer?" in English. You looked puzzled. When I finally understood, both of us just cracked into laughter.

Thank you for waking up my sleepy-head sons with William. I also remember we made gyoza dumpling together. You were very good at wrapping gyoza. Since I have only two sons who don't cook with me, the cooking experience with you made me feel like having a daughter. You were also fond of rice balls I made. It was only you, Grace, who complimented, "Auntie, you are a good cook." You are so sweet. Thank you for your compliment.

You tried out kimono when you were almost seven years old. I thought you were the prettiest of all, just like your mom. Whenever I see pretty dresses, shoes, and accessories, I find myself wondering whether they look good on you.

I wish I could have spent more time with you and done more for you. In coming spring your older cousin Ayumu moves out to Kyoto for graduate school, with memories of you and with the same lucky charm as you had, so he feels like you are always with him.

Please watch over all of us, Grace. I am very proud of being your aunt. Always think of you no matter where you are.

Yukiyo Matsumoto
Aunt in Japan

THIS SUMMER I TOOK A DRAWING CLASS

What are drawing classes? ... I didn't think it was so fun. I was one of the worst drawers in the class. I always messed up. The teacher always gave us drawing homework.

One day my drawing homework was to draw a dolphin. I drew it so well. I showed my mom and she was amazed! I showed my teacher, and she thought it was pretty good.

Now I don't think drawing lessons are so bad. After all, after you try it you don't think it is so bad.

HELLO, MY FUTURE TEACHERS

My name is Grace Makoto Tam, I am 11 years old. My mom is Japanese and my dad is Chinese, but I can only speak a little of the languages.

In kindergarten I went to Bethlehem Christian School (a private school). For first grade through fifth grade I went to Kellogg Marsh Elementary School. They are both in Marysville.

I have one little brother who is 9 and he goes to Kellogg Marsh Elementary.

I am usually very quiet on the first day of school, but I get more louder once I get used to the school. I like to have at least some friends to hang out with.

I do Kung Fu and piano. I also like to draw and I want to learn more about drawing skills. My favorite subject is writing, reading and art. I like to usually write on a certain subject, like fantasy and realistic fiction. I like to read books that are interesting, realistic, and fantasy. Art really interests me. I want to learn and become more better at my art skills.

A LETTER FROM MRS. BEASON

Grace will forever be remembered and missed. She was a beautiful person inside and out, and her smile made me smile. I was privileged to be one of her teachers. An excellent student, always eager to learn, she was a joy to teach. Grace had many gifts and was so willing to share them with those around her. Her kindness made her a favorite friend to many. She knew intuitively when others were hurting or anxious and quietly offered her support in whatever way they needed it. Grace was humble, never bragging or showing off her knowledge, even though her skills and understanding were often far above others in the classroom. Because she was selfless and so giving, I often thought what a marvelous teacher or doctor she would make.

In the years after I had Grace in second grade, she often appeared in my classroom doorway in the afternoon asking softly, "Do you need any help today?"

I looked forward to seeing her and gladly asked her to help with tutoring students in math or reading. Of course, *all* the students wanted

Grace's help! She always seemed embarrassed about that. With patience and compassion, she guided and encouraged each one.

Thank you, Grace, for giving us all such wonderful memories. What an amazing blessing it is to be one of the many, many people forever touched by Grace's love.

Carol Beason
Second grade teacher

TRIPS AND TRAVELING

I love traveling on vacation. Last year first I went to Mexico. Then I went to Japan. Now this year I am going to Hawaii. Almost every year we go on two vacations a year. In second grade I went to Hawaii and China and Japan. In third grade I went to Disneyland.

My favorite trip was to Hong Kong and Japan. I keep begging my mom if we could move to Japan. But she says it won't be fair for my dad. My dad really wants to move to Hawaii, but we haven't decided yet.

The airplane rides are so long and I don't really like riding on airplanes. But when we get there, I just want to go in the pool. I could stay in the pool for a long time. In Mexico I saw so many people selling on the streets. Even kids. It was really really sad.

Sometimes it's nice to be home.

WHENEVER I AM WITH SUGAR I FEEL HAPPY

Whenever I had a bad day or I am crying, I always look up to my dog. Even if I am mad, I still love her. But sometimes if she is naughty or she bites someone I get mad at her. But other than that there are not so many reasons I would be mad at her. I always try to smile at her and look happy. When I come home, I say hi to her. I ask her, "How was your day?"

She just keeps wagging her tail and jumping on me. She starts licking my face and that makes me very happy. The best place for me is to be with my dog in my room laying on pillows and reading. I am very glad I have my dog Sugar.

A Letter from Megan Sparr

Grace was one of my first and best friends when we moved out to Kayla's Glen. We met at school around kindergarten or first grade. We loved animals and because of that, we were going to open our own shelter together. We loved searching for frogs and snakes at the retaining pond. We both liked to ride dirt bikes and ATVs on my track. I also enjoyed going to her house to play with her dog and play Mario Kart on the Wii. I will miss her so much.

Sincerely,
Your friend always,
Megan Sparr
Friend

THE GREATEST THING I LEARNED THIS YEAR

1. Teamwork and to cooperate with others
2. Don't say good-bye because you never know if you will see them again
3. How to handle changes
4. What a true friend is (friendship)
5. You can do anything if you believe in yourself
6. Making new friends
7. To be more creative in writing and drawing
8. If you work hard, you will achieve
9. How to build a shelter
10. Just because someone looks pretty that doesn't mean they are nice

A Letter from Mr. Doup

Always with a calm demeanor and gentle smile, Grace worked to grow and improve.

Many people outside of China think Kung Fu means martial arts. Kung Fu, in fact, refers to a high level of achievement in any skill that takes lots of time and practice to achieve. You can have Kung Fu in martial arts, cooking, or violin. To achieve Kung Fu takes time, discipline, and hard work. Grace had the discipline. She was also no stranger to hard work. The only thing Grace didn't have was enough time.

Earning a black belt is not just about punching fast and kicking high. It is about being a good person. It is about cultivating discipline, respect, and humility. It is about having a strong work ethic and a "nothing is impossible" attitude. Grace Tam was the embodiment of all these things.

In our school, as a reminder to all of our students, hangs a black belt that Grace surely would have worn if only she had enough time.

Sifu Carlton Doup
Kung Fu Teacher

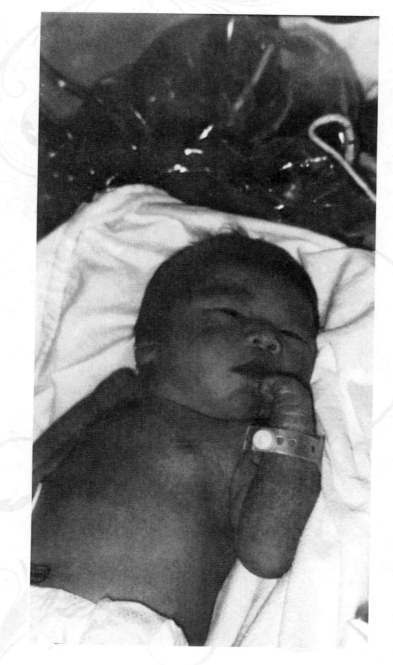

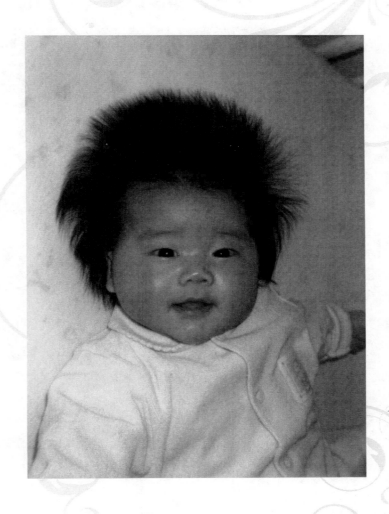

July 2010

August 2010

November 2010

GRACE MAKOTO TAM
With John Tam and Tamami Okauchi

February 2010

THE GREATEST THING YOU LEARNED THIS YEAR

When I was visiting Japan, I said good-bye and then I thought good-bye means you will never see them again. So I learned do not say good-bye. You will see them again.

I learned you need to handle the change, like when Natalie Jumaoas move to Rhode Island, I knew I had to handle the change.

Making new friends was very hard for me at the beginning of the school year. Everyone was silent in class and that made me nervous of making new friends. Then one day Mr. Daoust said pick someone to play a math game with you have never met. So I went over to a girl named Carrie. We started playing together. At first we were quiet, then we started talking to each other about ourselves. At recess we started playing with each other. Now me and her are the best friends.

A Letter from Natalie Jumaoas

My friendship with Grace was very important to me and still is.

The first day of school she was in 5th grade and I was in 4th. I remember she was a very quiet but sweet and kind girl. She was nice to everyone and she was very funny, too.

The more time I spent with Grace I found things that we had in common. My time that I spent with her was very short but it was valuable and worth it.

I don't remember the things she said but the thing that I will never forget is "Why do you have to go?" on the last day I had to move. After that I wanted to stay even more.

My relationship with Grace was very important to me. We would contact each other by mostly email. She would tell a lot of things from her enjoyable trip to what she got for Christmas. Since then I have saved those emails and will keep them forever.

After I heard the dreadful tragedy I was heartbroken. I couldn't believe it, but I wished I was there to see her before the tragedy.

As I saw the pictures of her it brought back so many memories. I had just lost one of my friends.

It was hard to hear what happened but I will never forget her.

Prayers sent from Natalie all the way from Rhode island. Love, Natalie

Natalie Jumaoas
Friend

ARE WISHES WHAT YOU WANT?

One night I was out on my room balcony, and I saw a shooting star. I was very amazed. So I decided I was going to make a wish that I've always wanted to wish. I wished I was very rich. I knew it wouldn't come true, but I still had hope for my wish to come true. So that night I went to bed and thought about my wish very hard, because I really wanted my wish to come true. After a couple minutes my mom came and said goodnight to me.

"Do you think, if you wish on a shooting star, your wish will come true?" I asked my mom.

"Maybe, but you never know," my mom replied.

I fell asleep at around 10 o'clock P.M., hoping for my wish to come true.

The next morning I woke to my alarm, I think, but it was actually a bell from up above me. I looked around me. I was in a purple king-sized bed! My room had a pool in it! *Had my wish come true?* I wondered. I got out of my bed and explored the house. My house was like a mansion! Every room was filled with fancy furniture. On the outside it said my first and last name. I was not in my same neighborhood.

Where are my parents? I wondered.

"Where are my parents?" I asked one of my servants.

"They are not here because you are rich, and you don't need them," my servant explained.

My servants were all wearing pink and purple clothes that said, "Working for Grace Tam."

I was only 11 years old and had no parents! I had blackish reddish hair and dark brown eyes. I loved puppies and dogs, and I liked writing stories. *May be my dog Sugar is here,* I wondered. Aha! She was in my room!

"Oh, Sugar, do you know where am I?" I asked her.

She was sort of snobby though. Sugar had black fur and a little white spot on her chest. She only weighed 15 pounds. Even though I didn't know what type of dog Sugar was, I still loved her so much and thought she was one on the cutest dogs.

Ding Dong! The doorbell rang. *Maybe it is my parents,* I wondered. A girl who looked like me was at the door.

"Hi, my name is Carrie Cha," the girl cheerfully said to me.

"Hi," I replied nervously.

"Can you help me to figure out where I am?" I asked Carrie.

"Of course!" Carrie cheerfully said.

"Can I spend the night?" Carrie asked.

"Sure," I said still sounding nervous. *This is very strange,* I thought.

"I like cats, and my favorite color is lime green! I also like writing stories," Carrie said to me.

"Where do you live?" I asked Carrie.

"Across from you," Carrie explained.

Carrie was as not rich as me, but she had parents. Carrie also explained to me that the girl who lived next door was very mean and snobby. She also explained that I lived on Sunny Side Street in California. My house was in Washington. So me and Carrie went to the house next door to me.

A girl who looked familiar answered the door.

"Mikayla?" I questioned the girl.

Mikayla had brown hair, greenish eyes, and lots of makeup on. I had to admit she was very pretty. Carrie had blackish reddish hair like me, dark brown eyes and she wasn't as girly as Mikayla.

"Ehew!" Mikayla shouted while spitting in me and Carrie's faces. "Get out of here!" Mikayla shouted in my face.

"Why?" I asked Mikayla.

"I used to be the only one rich; then you appeared!" Mikayla yelled louder at me and Carrie's faces.

Me and Carrie got very sad and went back to my house for the sleepover.

"Wow your house is huge!" Carrie said, sounding surprised.

"Is Mikayla always that mean and rude to other people?" I asked Carrie.

"Yes. She always spreads rumors about me and bullies other people." Carrie replied, sounding sad.

"Well, this time I am not going to let that happen!" I said, sounding brave.

Me and Carrie ate spaghetti and garlic bread sticks. Both of our favorites! We had lots more in common than I expected.

"Can I tell you a secret?" I asked Carrie while we were eating.

"Yeah," Carrie replied with a mouthful of spaghetti.

"The truth is, I wished on a shooting star that I was very rich and that's why I am rich," I explained to Carrie.

"Do you like being rich and having no parents?" Carrie asked.

"I like being rich, but I miss having parents," I told her. "Do you believe me?" I asked Carrie.

"Yes, because you are my friend," Carrie answered.

After staying up and watch movies, Carrie and I went to bed.

In the morning, Carrie, still lying in bed, was not awake yet. Then something shiny and gold, like a fairy, appeared.

"Hello, I am Hayli, the fairy of wishes," Hayli said. "I made your wish come true," Hayli explained. "I will come back tomorrow morning to see if you want your wish to be redone," Hayli whispered.

Hayli had a white silk dress on with a crown on. She held a wand in her hand, and she could fly in the sky. After I told Hayli I didn't want to redo my wish, she drifted off in the sky. In a couple of minutes, Carrie woke up. I told her about Hayli, the wish fairy. She believed me, but she didn't want me to go because she wanted me to get rid of Mikayla. I told her I wasn't going to redo my wish yet until I defeated evil Mikayla.

"I love your room," Carrie said, sounding surprised.

My rich room had purple paint on the wall; it also had a big indoor pool.

"I wish I was as rich as you, but have parents," Carrie said while yawning.

Me and Carrie had breakfast and got dressed quickly so we could go spy or make Mikayla stop bulling other people. My closet was *ginormous* and had a ton of cute clothes. I let Carrie borrow some clothes too.

After we got dressed me and Carrie went to see Mikayla. Mikayla answered the door and shouted "What do you want?"

Mikayla's friend Kayci was there too. Kayci had blonde hair and blue eyes.

"There are two of them now," I whispered in Carrie's ear.

"Why are you always mean to me?" I asked Mikayla.

"Because I used to be the only one rich and popular at our school, then you appeared and ruined my popular crowd with Kayci," Mikayla said, sounding angry.

"Yeah," Kayci said after Mikayla.

"It's not my fault!" I yelled at Mikayla with my mouth wide open.

"I'm gonna tell my mom!" I yelled. Then I remembered I was rich and I had no parents. I sighed really big. Now what was I going to do.

I thought. "Okay, me and you are going to have a bet of president of our school. The looser has to move out and live homeless as the rest of the life," I said, sounding greedy.

"Deal," Mikayla and Kayci yelled in me and Carrie's faces.

Me and Carrie walked back to my house and made posters for me to be president.

"How am I going to win the bet?" I asked Carrie, hoping for an answer.

"I am thinking about it," Carrie whispered.

That night Hayli came, and I told her I didn't want to redo my wish yet.

"Okay. I will be back tomorrow and see if you want your wish to be redone," Hayli replied.

The next morning, I went to Kent Moore Middle School. Me and Carrie rode in my limo to school. We hung up posters for me to be president of our school.

"I'm really nervous for the vote," I whispered in Carrie's ear.

"Don't worry. I am going to get you better grades than Mikayla," Carrie whispered back to me.

"Oh, look who it is!" Mikayla snapped while taking off her 10 million dollar sunglasses. A huge crowd surrounded Mikayla.

Oh no, I thought.

When we got home, me and Carrie looked how many votes I had and how many votes the monster had (Mikayla). When we looked on the computer, we figured out I had three less votes than Mikayla had. The next day I got an A+ on my math test, but I got a D- on my English test.

"Mikayla is one vote ahead of you," Carrie said, sounding surprised.

The decision who was president of our school was next week. I was very scared and nervous of the bet. I wondered if Mikayla was going to win. That week went very slow. Hayli came every night, and I told her I didn't want to redo my wish yet.

Finally it was time to announce the winner of president of our school. I had butterflies fluttering in my stomach. I watched the words come out of the principal's mouth.

"Grace Tam is president of Kent Moore Middle School," the principal said loudly in the microphone.

"You won, Grace!" Carrie shouted.

Me and Carrie hugged for a long time.

"You are one of the best friends ever!" I said, sounding happy.

When we got home, me and Carrie told Mikayla she had to move out and live as a homeless person for the rest of her life.

"Nnnnnooooo!" Mikayla yelled at the top of her lung.

So Mikayla and Kayci moved out. Kayci also moved out because she was part of the bet. Me and Carrie were as happy as can be!

When I got home, I said, "Mom, aren't you proud I got president?" Then I remembered I had no parents, and I wanted to go back to my real world.

"Hayli!" I shouted.

"Yes," Hayli replied, while coming through the window.

"I want to redo my wish," I said. "Wait, let me say good-bye to Carrie," I said, while walking to Carrie's house.

"Good-bye, Carrie," I said sounding very sad.

"You are my best friend," Carrie said.

Me and Carrie hugged, and I went to my house.

"Hayli, I'm ready," I said.

The next morning I woke up by the smell of frying bacon. *Was that a dream?* I thought. I walked downstairs and saw my mom.

"Mom!" I said, while hugging her so tight.

"It's just me, your mom," My mom said sounding confused.

I told her what happened, but she didn't believe me. My mom had blackish reddish hair same as me, dark brown eyes, and she always had a smile on her face. Sugar was there too, and she was not snobby anymore. That whole day was Sunday, so I stayed home and spent time with my family. I felt happy where I was now.

The next day I went to school, and Carrie was a new student in our class! Carrie looked just the way she did in my rich world. I was very amazed and surprised! Mikayla was there, and she was nice to me! At recess I talked to Carrie to see if she wanted to be friends. Carrie told me, "I like cats and my favorite color is lime green. I also like writing stories."

When I heard what Carrie said, I couldn't believe my ears. From that day on, I learned my lesson that I like where I live, and you don't have to be rich to be happy. I also learned parents are more important than being very rich.

JELLYFISH STING

There once was a day when I got stung by jellyfish. It was a painful and funny memory.

Me and my family were in Mexico traveling. We decided to take a boat (a tour), and you can swim in the water and look at fish. The boat was starting, and I was kind of nervous. I was kind of cold, and my teeth were chattering. I was nervous of swimming in the water. Me and my family started taking pictures of things we saw.

The boat stopped, and I started getting my life vest and my snorkel on. First I swam with my mom. The water felt good, because it was steaming hot outside.

"Come over here. You can see a lot more," my mom called over the water.

"No, thanks, I'm good," I replied back to my mom.

I swam and saw lots of fish. There was yellow, orange, blue, and all sorts of colors. I was kind of scared, but at least I am much braver than my brother. My mom thought my dad should come out, so he did.

"Do you like the boat ride so far?" my dad asked.

"Yeah, it is quite fun," I said, sounding not so excited.

"Good, I am glad you are enjoying the boat ride," my dad replied.

We swam and looked at more fish. I was starting to think I was actually getting the hang of it. Something was bothering my leg.

"Aaaaaaahhhhhh!!!" I screamed so loud that my throat started to hurt. My dad pulled me to shore and looked at my leg. Almost half my leg looked red, with scratches on my leg. *How will I ever get back to the boat?* I thought. I was panicking very bad. A family heard me crying and asked if I was okay.

"Calm down. You are okay," my dad said, trying to sound like everything was going to be okay, but I thought nothing was going to be okay. One of the family members came over to me and said he will try to get me back to the boat. While he got me back to the boat, he asked about me. I was wondering if my dad would come back to the boat.

When I got back to the boat, everyone was staring at me. I was kind of embarrassed. My mom thanked the guy for bringing me back. My dad actually ended up on the wrong boat. On the way back, they served a really good meal. They served us Mexican rice, vegetables, and some other good stuff. I was very quiet on the way home. On the way back, they got a hose, and we got to wash off the sea water. It felt better. I was thinking, I was only 10 years old, and I already got stung by jellyfish. We saw whales on the way back, they were really big, but we only saw some part.

When we got back, I felt like I accomplished a big adventure! I didn't know what to say when we were driving back. My leg was filled with scars. It hurt still badly. From that day on I learned my lesson not to panic so bad and worry. It will make it worse. Now when it has become a memory, it seems funny how on the way there I seemed excited, but on the way back I looked very gloomy.

MY SWEET DOG SUGAR

One day my mom said we were going to go see dogs.

"Are we going to get a dog?"

"You'll see."

I kept jumping up and down, because I was so exited!

I asked my mom, "Where are we going?"

"To a shelter," she said.

After a couple days, which seemed like forever we went to the shelter. When I was out of the car, two dogs came over to me and jumped on me. They were so adorable! My mom asked the lady to bring out Penny. She said, "Sure."

Penny was very scared and shy. Emma and Minnie were way too wild.

My mom said, "So, what do you think?"

We had a choice to get Emma or Penny. Minnie was too old. I said I wanted Penny, and my brother said he wanted Penny. Everyone agreed to get Penny, so we told the lady. My mom and dad paid, then we got Penny!

We put her in the car, and we started thinking of a name for her. Since we got her close to Valentine's Day, we wanted to name something sweet. She also had a white spot on her chest. So we decided to name her Sugar. I was so happy!

"Mom and Dad, thank you!"

"You're welcome!"

Now that Sugar is our dog, everyone loves Sugar. Sugar is ours, and she knows her name, and she loves us a lot. I am happy to have Sugar as our dog.

A LETTER FROM MRS. CAMPBELL

I met Tamami at my yoga class. We discovered that we lived in the same neighborhood. Over time I heard about her two children, Grace and William.

She heard that I was a piano teacher. She was interested in having Grace learn about the piano. I think Grace was in second grade when she started piano in the fall of 2006. She was very shy and quiet. She did not want to be in recitals or play for anyone, but her Mom kept encouraging her. We did some duets at the recitals to make it more comfortable.

When she would come for her lesson, she would hug her mom tightly. I often wondered if she did not want to have the piano lessons, but once she sat on the piano bench, she tried everything I asked of her. We would do something new each week and she would say, "That's so hard!" Then we would work on it and she would be able to do it. We would look back at things she thought were hard and she would see that now they were easy. As time went on, she became more interested and played by herself in the recitals. She started to gain some skill at playing and even asked me questions at the lessons. She related to Disney tunes and Hannah Montana, which is pretty normal for her age. I found a music book of Chinese Folk songs arranged for the piano. I was hoping to explore those with her to see a little of her Chinese heritage. We tried to find Japanese music also, but it was a little more advanced level and would require a little more skill.

One year, she came for her lessons and seemed quite upset. She told me that her mom wanted to get rid of the dog they had just gotten. It was a big black dog that chewed things a lot and was hard to handle. But Grace's heart was broken. We talked about how life is hard sometimes and it helps to have a friend who can help you feel better. Shortly after that her mom was very ill and I could tell she was afraid. I tried to reassure her that her mom would get better and that she loved her very much. She knew that. I think their family became very close that year. One day after her mom recovered, Grace came to her lesson all excited. They had found a new dog. It was a small black dog, and Grace named her "Sugar."

Grace enjoyed the latest fashions for girls. But she always used good taste and had appropriate selections to wear. She often had fingernail polish. One day she and her friends even painted Sugar's toenails.

Her family rode their bikes to our place one summer day and picked peas in our garden. She was very curious and got the hang of it. That was a good day.

I will always remember Grace as a sweet girl. She had the nature of an angel. In my mind she will always be the picture of a beautiful innocent eleven-year-old girl. But I like to think of her now as a complete person—a true angel with God— radiating her love to us. The music she "sings" is love. She now understands all that God intended for her at any age. Her inner beauty is everlasting and will be with me forever.

Jane Campbell
Piano teacher

THE ELIAN GONZALEZ STORY

November 1999, Thanksgiving a little boy was found in water almost drowned. Almost died, but he survived. A miracle!

His mother wanted him to start over. She wanted him to be back the USA traveling in a small boat. There was a big storm. The boat began to sink. His mother and the fisherman drowned.

The boy was safe but scared. They don't want him to go to Cuba.

People surrounded Elian's house. Cops and helicopters surrounded Elian's house. Someone needs to make a decision to make him go to Cuba or United States.

She decided to make him go to Cuba with his father. But the people didn't want him to. They will not give up Elian.

April 22, 2000, she sent people to Elian's house. Soon he was on the plane. There were lots of newspapers of Elian. Elian's father was very happy to see him. Elian has gone through a lot. He wants to have a normal life.

Every kid deserves to have a good childhood and at least a mother or father.

I think this because Elian had almost drowned, and he deserved to get his mother back, but his mother drowned so he deserves to go to his father. His relatives didn't want him to go back to his father. People shouldn't tell you what to do.

THE MYSTERY OF
THE ISLAND

In 1848, the twins named Kylie and Kyle were lying in bed when their mother came over to them to tuck them in. Their mother came to tell them that they were going to sail to America with their father tomorrow. Kylie and Kyle felt scared and nervous.

Finally Kyle had the nerve to speak up, "But why, Mother?" Kyle asked.

"Because," said their mother and turned out the light.

"Why do you think we have to leave?" said Kylie.

"I really don't know," said Kyle.

The next morning Kylie and Kyle had to wake up early to go on their trip. They crept downstairs quietly so their mother and father couldn't hear them.

"Why should Kylie and Kyle go?" their father shouted quiet enough not to disturb the house.

"I want Kylie and Kyle to be free and to explore a new world," their mother replied.

"Do you want our only children to be sick and die from some kind of sickness like the others?" their father shouted loudly this time. Lottie and Nick raised their heads. Lottie and Nick were both sheepdogs. Kylie showed Kyle a scared and worried look, then quickly ran upstairs. Kyle followed behind.

After a little while Kyle and Kylie's mother came to get them ready. They were all packed up. Their father was waiting outside for them. He didn't have a happy face though. Kyle was packing toys so he didn't get bored on the ship. Meanwhile the mother curled Kylie's brown hair.

"You have beautiful green eyes," said the mother.

Kylie and Kyle didn't reply. Kylie didn't want to disappoint her mother so she forced an awkward smile. Soon they were ready to go. Their mother kissed them on the cheek good-bye. They were already on their way to America.

They boarded the ship and got taken to a room where kids were. This was where they were going to be most of the time. Kylie and Kyle were nervous. It was their first ride on a ship. Usually Kylie kept getting seasick. One stormy night

Kylie and Kyle stayed up late. Rain clattered on the outside of the ship. The boat sounded hollow as the rain clattered on the outside.

"I'm worried about Dad," Kylie said sounding scared as her voice echoed in the room. Kylie and Kyle felt uncomfortable and not safe. The only light they had as the moonlight through their window. They only had one candle that blew out hours ago. The room was full of bunk beds. Half an hour later they fell asleep. They both dreamed that they were both being back in England and everything was back to normal.

The next morning they woke up and went upstairs to see their father. It was the first time the sun shone ever since the ship left England. They quietly sneak up on the deck. Kylie and Kyle were not allowed on the deck, but they didn't know that. Before they could get into trouble from the captain, a sailor spotted them and scolded them and took them back into the children's room. When they got back they were not happy.

"Now how will we get to father?" Kyle asked Kylie.

"We'll find a way," Kylie said, sounding positive enough to convince Kyle. Kyle forced an awkward smile to make Kylie happy and looked convinced, but he still thought they'd never see their dad again. Who knows what could happen.

It has been 3 months since Kylie and Kyle came aboard.

Suddenly a sailor shouted, "Land Ho!"

Kylie and Kyle were overjoyed and so was everyone on the boat. Kylie and Kyle looked out the window, and they finally saw a light of sun. Suddenly Kylie and Kyle's dad spotted dark clouds heading their way.

"Storm ahead!" he yelled out loud, but everyone was too overjoyed to pay attention. Suddenly lightning streaked out from the sky, and everyone screamed so loud that it echoed the sky. The wind started to blow the ship to a different direction. Kylie and Kyle were searching everywhere for their father.

"Father!" Kylie and Kyle shouted over the ship.

"Don't panic!" Kylie shouted in her head. Kylie and Kyle couldn't find their dad. It was too big of a crowd to see through.

"Are you Derek's kids?" A sailor asked, looked like he was panicking very bad.

"Yes," Kylie and Kyle said with a worried look on.

"This way please!" the sailor said, while walking toward the front of the boat. Kylie and Kyle followed with worried looks on.

"Sir, I believe these are your kids," the sailor explained.

Without saying a word their father took them and guided them to his room. A big gush of wind moved the boat again.

"I want you to stay here for now. I don't want you to get hurt. Understand?" their father said while getting ready to leave.

"Yes, Father," Kylie and Kyle replied with a worried tone in their voice. Their father left and everything was sounds of screaming and yelling. Kylie and Kyle felt uncomfortable with all the noise. Eventually they fell asleep, with nightmares.

The next morning they awoke to lightning and thunder. Their father was nowhere to be seen. Without following the rules, they sneaked outside of the room to see what was going on.

"Where's father?" Kyle asked with a trembling voice.

"I have no clue." Kyle muttered with a look like he was going to cry. No one was on the boat except for Kylie and Kyle. The boat was sort of wrecked and looked like a huge storm had hit it. A plank was left that connected to an island.

"Let's go over there," Kylie suggested, trying to sound positive.

"It's worth a try, I guess," Kyle said, staring everywhere.

Kylie and Kyle walked together like two marshmallows stuck together. The island was mainly covered with forest and looked hard to survive in.

"Father has got to be here somewhere," Kyle said.

"It looks kind of impossible to find him in this forest," Kylie said, staring into the huge forest. Kylie and Kyle started looking around for their father.

Kylie and Kyle have been searching everywhere for their father for whole one hour. Finally they got so tired that they fainted. They both set a camp area up with sticks and a fire. After a long silence Kylie had breathe to speak.

"Will we ever find Father?" Kylie asked, while wiping a tear down her cheek.

"I don't know," Kyle replied, hugging his sister. Even though Kylie and Kyle had nothing to eat they tried not to complain.

"Good night," Kylie whispered, while closing her eyes.

"Good night to you, too," Kyle whispered back.

The next chilly morning Kylie and Kyle's father was there with them.

"Father!" Kylie and Kyle yelled with joy.

"Where were you?" Kyle asked while hugging his father.

"I traveled to land on the plank, and the next morning I remembered about you guys, and when I went back, no one was there," Kylie and Kyle's dad replied.

"Sorry. We ran away. We were worried about you," Kylie and Kyle muttered.

"Your mother should have never sent you on this ship." Kylie and Kyle's father said with an unhappy face on.

"Where is everyone else on the boat?" Kylie asked.

"Well, at nighttime when you were in the ship, the storm got worse and I managed to escape, but everyone else disappeared somewhere." Kylie and Kyle's father said with a sad face on. They stood quiet for a while and looked around. Kylie shot Kyle a what-should-we-do look. Kyle gave an I-don't-know look back.

EMALINE

Emaline is 6 years old, and she acts just like a princess. She is quite bossy. She thinks she is in charge. Emaline loves fashionable clothes and purses. Her room is like a castle. Her bed is huge. Her closet is full of dresses. Emaline is very picky with her food. Pink is her theme color. She is very annoying to her sister. Emaline is VERY spoiled. She always has to have pink on herself. Emaline always messes with her mom's makeup. She still doesn't know how to act lady like. Emaline can get away with everything. Her dream is to own a castle and be the princess.

A Letter from Mrs. Bierer

From the first time I saw Grace, she was just in kindergarten with my daughter, Ashley, nephew, Cameron, and family friend, Carter. Whenever my sister-in-law and I were talking about the other children in Mrs. Ramich's class, we would refer to Grace as the beautiful little girl with the adorable hair. Ashley's memories of Grace back then don't differ much at all from the Grace I came to know when I had her in fourth grade. Ashley said Grace was the very quiet one who always did the right thing and that she was good at "pretty much everything." When I found out in the fall before Grace's fourth grade year that she was going to be in my class, I was excited and a little sad at the same time. Of course I was thrilled to have Grace in my class, but having Grace was also a reminder of how quickly time passes, that my little Ashley, like Grace, was no longer a little girl. I can't help but think of song lyrics when reminiscing about days gone by or people we cherish. It makes me think of the song entitled "Don't Blink" with the obvious message that life is short, that it passes by more quickly than we can ever describe, far too early for some, for the very best it seems.

As I think back to having in Grace in class, I know that the Grace I knew is the same special girl that everyone knew. She was quiet, and humble, beautiful, and brilliant. She was way beyond her years in maturity . . . innocent but very intuitive and witty. She definitely was one of those kids who just "got it," and as her teacher, I knew right away that she was special (as I'm quite sure all of her previous teachers knew as well).

I remember one specific incident where there was a misunderstanding with a group of girls in class. Grace approached me and asked if we could all go sit down and discuss what was going on out at recess. She was very articulate, had described from her point of view (which was very accurate by the way, after having spoken with the other girls), what had happened, and how she had tried to resolve it on her own but that she had been unsuccessful. I remember thinking at the time that there are a lot of adults in the world who are incapable of handling complicated relationship issues so gracefully and yet here is this nine-year-old, effortlessly making a solid, heartfelt attempt to solve the problems of the world.

Grace was the child that every parent strives to raise. She was brilliant and humble, quiet but truly fearless. The beauty she possessed was clear to anyone who saw her, but even clearer to those who knew her. For those who were blessed enough to have had crossed paths with her in her short life, they knew that the most incredible beauty that she possessed was on the inside. As parents, the death of a child is unimaginable. It is so difficult to understand why things happen as they do in life.

I believe that Grace fulfilled her purpose on earth before she had a chance to grow old. She understood what life was about and had a heart that was so filled with love that God brought her home to the beauty that she deserved. Most take a lifetime what she achieved in a few short years. Her beautiful heart is a testament to the love that her parents nourished. Her loving spirit will live on for all of eternity.

Mrs. Bierer
Fourth grade teacher

MADISON

Madison is 12 years old, and she is Emaline's sister. She loves dogs, and she is very kind. She doesn't get along with her sister though. She loves texting and working on her laptop computer. Her room isn't so flashy. She loves hot pink and magenta and lime green. She has envy of her sister. She still likes makeup and purses. She likes clothes and getting her nails done. She is not a princess though. Her bed and bedroom is very big and nice. She knows how to act ladylike and how to act kind to other people. Whenever her sister is bugging her, she is the one who gets in trouble. Her dream is to own a mansion, and she will have a shelter for dogs. Her nightmare is her sister.

MY BROTHER
BOTHERING ME!!!!!

One day my mom was pregnant, and she had a baby. I was only two years old, and I didn't know what was going on.

Several years passed and my brother is very annoying. We have gotten into so many fights. I can't count them all. Once I was playing with my mom, and my brother spilled juice on me on purpose! But lucky for me, he got in huge trouble.

Once I was studying doing my homework and he kept bothering me and I told him to stop, but he still did it when my mom came home. We both told her and she asked what was wrong. I said, "William is bothering me," and then my brother came out and said I was yelling at him, when I never was! My mom said me and my brother would have no TV time for today. I was very mad because it wasn't my fault!

Now you see why he is annoying! (Not always true.) Sometimes nice! Only!

A Letter from William

Dear Grace,

When you passed away I never thought that good-byes could come so soon.

Here are some things you should know about Grace.

Grace and I kept getting in fights. She would accuse me for starting the fight when she really started it.

She would start it but when my parents heard us she said that I started it. She would say, "He just started arguing."

But Grace can sometimes be nice. Sometimes only!

But there are some things we liked to do together. We liked to play with our cousins. We also liked to play with our dog, Sugar.

If Grace were here with me again, I wouldn't have so many arguments with her, and I would tell her I love her.

William

POEMS

Poems are fun to write
Sometimes they are peaceful
And sometimes they give you all right!
But whatever you write
Don't give up and write at daylight!

CARRIE

*C*aring to others
A really good friend
*R*eally kind to me
*R*espectful to her family
*I*n a good mood
*E*njoying to have around

A Letter from Carrie

My name is Carrie Cha and I was a student at Kellogg Marsh elementary school. It was the first day of school and I was really nervous. My teacher was Mr. Daoust and he was my first male teacher. When I got there I didn't know anyone. The day started out with us introducing each other. It felt really uncomfortable at first, but then I got used to it.

A couple of weeks later, our class was playing math games. I was partners with a girl named Grace Tam. She was Chinese and Japanese. Her favorite color was purple. She played the piano and took Kung Fu lessons. She was also very smart. She loved puppies a lot too. I am Thai ad Hmong. My favorite color is also purple, blue, and lime green. I want to learn how to play the guitar and I am really good at drawing. I am also smart, but not very smart. I prefer cats over dogs. Grace and I became best friends. We did everything together.

It was the first week of October, when finally the leaves started to change color. My birthday was coming up and so was Halloween. The weather was getting colder. During the first couple of weeks of October our class was drawing, writing, and creating all kinds of stuff. Most of us were also improving on math and reading. During recess Grace and I talked about what we were going to be for Halloween.

She said, "I'm going to be Dorothy from *the Wizard of Oz.*"

"I don't know what I'm going to be yet," I said. Finally the bell rang. It was time for lunch. It seemed as if Grace always had cold lunch and I had sometimes hot lunch.

Finally my birthday came. I was so excited. Then I realized that I didn't invite Grace.

My mom then said, "It's okay, Carrie, you can go to the movies with her someday,"

"Okay," I said.

So the party went well and I was also wondering what Grace was doing.

After a couple weeks later it was Halloween and I was a witch. I had a black dress and a black hat. Grace was Dorothy like she said she was going to be. Her hair was braided and she had red shoes and a basket with a dog. She also had a blue dress on. Grace was really nervous and so was I. School finally ended. Darkness followed behind. It was trick-or-treats time and I went to every house. By the time my brother and sister and I got back home, my feet were aching. Grace was probably enjoying herself to treats at home. Before I went to bed I had to brush my teeth and clean up and change. Tomorrow was school so my brother and sisters and I had to got to bed at 9:00. Before I went to bed I thought about what Grace was doing. Then I fell asleep. The next morning I got up and got dressed and everything. I had breakfast and then I went to wait for the bus. The bus came and my little brother and my younger sister and I got on the bus. The bus went to other stops as usual. Finally we got to school. I waited till Grace's bus came. Her bus came and we ran to each other.

"Grace, did you get a lot of candy for Halloween?" I said.

"Yeah I did, but it's really sweet and probably too much candy for me to eat," she said.

Those were the best times I had with Grace. She was kind, sweet, honest, and caring. I could make a whole list of what Grace was like. When I heard about the accident near the ice caves, I was really shocked and I didn't believe it at first. It was the worst day of my life. Since then I cannot stop thinking about her once. I still miss her a lot too. It was really very nice getting to know her and becoming her best friend. Grace was and will always be my best friend.

Carrie Cha
Friend

MR. DAOUST

*M*onster to me
*R*eally stinky like a rotten twinky
*D*eveloping evilness
A
O
U
*S*caring kids with his face
T

A Letter from Mr. Daoust

The start of a new school year always brings excitement. Last year was no exception. The first time I met Grace was no different. I first met Grace and her parents when they walked into the classroom at our open house prior to the start of the school year. My first impression of her was that she was extremely shy and very quiet. Right away I came up with three goals for her: to help her overcome her shyness, to speak louder, and to smile. We really were able to reach two goals, as Grace blossomed overcoming her shyness. At the start of the year, Grace was extremely nervous. This would explain why she wouldn't smile. As the year progressed, I cannot remember a day where she didn't smile. The last one, well as hard as we both tried, she could not be loud. It was not in her, so instead I would just stand close enough to hear her. One thing all my students, including Grace, have taught me is to take who they are and work with that.

From the first day of school to the last day, Grace always gave her best. She always wanted to get better. It didn't matter if it was at school or outside of school. There are so many examples that I could write about that shows how Grace accomplished this each and every day. It didn't matter if it was at school or outside of school. Grace always worked to be better.

That's the type of person Grace was. She always wanted to get better or do better. It wasn't just with school work. She put the same effort and approach into everything, working on her Kung Fu, playing the piano, or playing with her friends. I had a feeling that Grace would ask herself three questions. Is this good enough? How do I get better? How do I help you? Watching her grow throughout the school year, I now realize that these are the same three questions I need to ask each and every day.

As a teacher I have many memories of the students I have taught. There are some memories of students that stick with you longer than others. Grace is, and would have been, one of those students. I have several memories that will stay with me for a long time.

The first is seeing her every morning. I teach in a portable and the students line up along the ramp. Every morning Grace was there and would say "Good morning, Mr. Daoust." She loved going to school not only to learn, but to get better. She knew that she wanted to get better but also she wanted to make you get better as well.

Grace and her family would take trips, which brings me to my next memory. When students in my room take trips like this, I have them keep a journal of what they did on their trip. I then have a follow up conversation with them about the experience and what they may have learned. Grace kept an incredible journal of what she did and where she went. She even gave a good description of the plane rides they took to get there. (Little side note, she did not like flying and even got sick a couple of times). Grace also would talk about if she would like to live in the places they visited.

One of her trips took her to Hawaii. This was in the month of December. At that time of year, we were experiencing a bitter cold spell. When Grace returned we were still in that cold spell. The whole class was very excited that she was back. When I asked her if she wished that she was still there she simply replied, "Yeah, it's warm there!"

As we started our day, the students were working in their math journal. We had to go to PE, so I took the time to read her journal. I was reading about all the fun things they did as a family, when on the side I noticed some writing. Grace had taken the time to let me know how warm it really was there. On the side she wrote, Hawaii 85, Marysville 17. When I called her on it, she just smiled and said, "It was warm." In that smile you could see how much she had grown. She was now joking around in class when she had the opportunity.

Another time that comes to mind is Halloween. Grace came dressed as Dorothy from the *Wizard of Oz*. She was in complete character, from the pigtails to the blue and white dress and red ruby shoes. She even had a small basket that she kept with her all day.

Probably the biggest and greatest memory I have of Grace is how she would work with other students. Grace was always willing to listen to what they had to say or help them out anyway she could. There is one particular time that shows the type of person Grace was.

We were working on the Colonies and had a project that required students to work with a partner. Grace was working very hard to get her partners involved in the project. Unfortunately, her partner was having a hard time. As hard as she tried, her partner would not work with her. Instead they wanted to do it their own way. In the long run, it was Grace who did most of the work. When it came time for the presentation, her partner was acting like they had done all the work. While this was hard for Grace, she allowed the student to take the credit. When I asked her why, she simply stated that she just wanted the project done, even if it meant that she did all the work. I told her that I had seen how hard she worked trying to involve her partner and that sometimes the other person is not willing to work as hard. Grace just said she wanted them to get better and see how to work with other people. Grace was showing humility and integrity while dealing with a difficult partner.

By far, this is one of the hardest things I have ever had to write. As a teacher, I am the one who is supposed to teach. It takes a rare student or individual who is able to teach their teacher. Grace is, and will always be, one of those students. I have many memories of Grace, and all of them bring to mind two words: *respect* and *honor*. Grace showed that to everyone she came into contact with. She accepted each person in their individual uniqueness. Thank you, Grace, for re-teaching me this lesson.

Rest in peace, Grace. The person you were will help me teach other students what they can become.

Richard Daoust
Fifth grade teacher

PURPLE

*P*urple is pretty
*U*nique to look at
*R*eally stands out
*P*retty like purple flowers
*L*ike the end of a rainbow
*E*legant and noble

A Letter from the Pattison Family

We have been blessed to know Grace and her family for almost seven years. When we first moved into the neighborhood, my son was two and a half and my daughter was a newborn. John and Tamami were our first neighbors we met along with their kids, Grace and William. The funny thing is my daughter's name was going to be Grace because we loved Gracie, but at the last minute we changed her name to Chloe.

When we first met our new neighbors, I knew Grace was going to be a special person. She lit up the room and I knew then that *she* was meant to be a "Gracie."

Grace was the older kid in the neighborhood but was always willing to play with and teach the younger kids. My kids loved playing school with Grace; to this day, they will tell you that Grace was the *best* teacher in the world! Anytime they went to the Tams, they always came home with a special craft they made with Grace and William.

Chloe loved playing house with Grace and even though Grace was five years older, Chloe always convinced Grace to let her be the mom. That is one of the many things that made Grace special; she always wanted everyone to be happy.

William used to be afraid of our dog, Rocky, and Grace was always right there telling him, "It's okay . . . Rocky loves us!"

It didn't take long before Rocky was a fixture of the Tam's backyard! We have been truly blessed to have lived next door to Grace and her family. Grace not only taught my kids the value of being a good friend, but me as well. Gracie was truly a *great* person, and we will be forever thankful for knowing her. We will cherish the short time we had with her and know that we are better for knowing her. We are extremely honored and blessed to be able to share our experiences about Grace and only wish we could have more. Grace was a very special person and even though we miss her every day, God obviously knew he was getting the best when he brought Gracie Tam home! We miss and love you every day, Grace Tam!!

Love,
The Pattison Family
Neighbor

SNOW

Snowmen all over town
Nose cold
Outside having fun
White on the ground

January 2010

FLOWERS

Flowers are pretty and enjoying
Sometimes bees get very annoying
But flowers smell very good and
They make you in a good mood

April 2010

GREEN

Green is for St. Patrick's Day
Where you will see leprechauns
But they will hide away
So do that they say

A Letter from
the Neal Family

It is truly an honor that you have asked me to write down my memories of Grace. My family and I have lived across the street and have had the pleasure of knowing Grace for six years. We got to watch her grow from a very shy little girl into a mature, beautiful young lady. She had the most beautiful big brown eyes and the longest hair. She always reminded me of Pocahontas.

I have many fond memories of sweet Grace! Just a few are: the neighborhood birthday parties, the kids swimming in our hot tub during the summer, riding their bikes together in the cul-de-sac, and spending time at the pond catching bugs and tad poles.

She was a very special friend to my daughter, Kami. Most kids the age of Grace really wouldn't give a four or five-year-old the time of day. But Grace *did*. She was so patient with Kameryn, like an older sister would be.

Usually they would play school, house, Barbies, or Grace would give Kami a makeover. And I could always tell when Grace had been over to our house because a multi-level book shelf in the shape of a house in Kameryn's room would be totally transformed into a very highly decorated Barbie condo. I got such a kick out of it; it put a smile on my face every time. I had finally found another child who truly appreciated Barbie!

I would overhear her and Kameryn playing and she would giggle and say, "Oh, Kameryn," and then giggle some more. She said it so adoringly. It just melted my heart.

I will forever remember your infectious laugh, Grace; it echoes in my memories.

Missing you,
Stephanie Neal and family
Neighbor

LUNCH

Lunch is very yummy
As it goes into my tummy
I like the school lunch
And I like bunch

September 2010

MY FAMILY

My family is very caring.
They take care of me and feed me.
They try their best to make me happy.
Even if they are busy they play with me.
I am very happy to have a caring family.

A Letter from Aunt Ruth

As you watch over us from heaven, know that you are loved.

Every day, your "Uncle" Guy and I, "Aunt" Ruth, are reminded of you as we see our pets; it's something that you really enjoyed interacting with when you came to visit. You liked petting our cats and gathering chicken eggs, but we also see you in the flowers that grow in our garden and the peaches on our tree. You had such broad interests.

Even our own children, Devan, Tala, Lance, and Danika, remind us of you. Your beautiful face is so much like Danika that every time we look at her, we see you. The two of you will be forever like sisters for us. Lance too shares a similar age with you though Lance played more with William, we thought of you as "mates" as you were more similar in age. We will continue to foster the playmates in William and Lance. Tala will always share that quiet countenance that is you, while Devan will be the "big brother" you never had.

And finally, we think of you every time we say hello or good-bye to anyone. Though you were reserved upon greeting us, you would smile broadly and talk quietly. Even though we did not get to see you often, you were always so sad, crying when we had to part that it breaks my heart to remember the few good-byes we shared, making this final one even harder to bear.

All Our Love,
Aunt Ruth, Uncle Guy,
Devan, Tala, Lance, and Danika
Family

SHOES

They are comfy and warm
Not like sandals
Make your feet warm and
Get your feet out of the cold
Some are big, some are small
But you will need shoes all your life

MY DOG SUGAR

I love my dog Sugar.
All cuddly and warm.
She is black with a tiny white spot
on her warm black chest.
She can sometimes get difficult,
but I still love her even more.
We play and play,
all day long
With a huge smile on our faces,
and as happy as can be.
I am so glad
I have my dog Sugar

FRIENDS

Friends are very helpful
They protect you from bullies
Sometimes they help you with work
Friends give up their time for you
I like helpful friends
Friends usually have sleepovers
It is fun especially with your friends
They spend a lot of time with you
It makes a smile on your face
I like sleepovers with friends
What a friend is
A friend is a person you like
A person you like, for how they act to you
Not how that person looks
A friend is a person who is caring

A Letter from Jazmin Guzman

Grace was one of my best friends that passed away. She was a girl like no other. She liked people for who they were, and she wouldn't care if they were homeless or rich. And I will miss her so much just like most of you do. Now I think back to the past. It was nice to spend all of my third grade recess with her teaching her how to hit a tether ball so she would master it. She got pretty good and every time I think about that day I know she will always be here with all the ones she loves. I also know now she is an angel up in heaven and will never be forgotten.

Jazmin Guzman
Friend

PUPPIES

Puppies are very cute
Their noses are so small
Sometimes they twitch when they lick
Their cuteness brightens my day
I love cute puppies
Puppies have lots of energy, so they play a lot
They can entertain you all day
When you play with them, you feel joyful
You can take them to the bay to play
I hope I can play with my puppy
Puppies love to cuddle at night
They keep you company
When you have nightmares, they are there
You will not be frightened at night
So at daylight you can feel good!

GRACE, MY MOST FAVORITE GIRL

Grace was my most favorite girl in the world.

Grace will be my most favorite girl all the time.

Grace loved vulnerable dogs and people.

Grace took care of me as if I were her baby.

Grace made me feel safe when she was by me.

Grace pet and kissed me gently when I jumped on her laps.

Grace is a girl whom I will miss all the time.

Grace is a sweetest girl who will live in my heart for the rest of my life.

Grace, thank you very much for your love and sweetness.

Sophie,
a dachshund who loves Grace

ST. PATRICK'S DAY

Leprechauns! Leprechauns!
Running around the streets!
I hope they don't catch me!
With gold in their pockets,
Green on their shoes,
And trying not to be seen.
Gold! Gold!
I want gold!
You have to find it from the leprechauns.
Sneaking through the bushes.
Swimming in the pool,
Hoping to find a pot of gold.
Green is St. Patrick's Day color.
I wonder why it is.
Green everywhere.
You will find it here and there.
Make sure you wear green
On St. Patrick's Day!

A Letter from the Margo Family

There is no other name that would better fit this little girl.

She had grace in her manners.

She had grace in her walk.

She had grace in her view of the world.

Grace

Grace was a child who was always watching, interpreting, and analyzing. She was the daughter a parent would dream to have. She was obedient, yet she would challenge. She learned and questioned. She was willing to listen and then decide. She had such love in her heart for her family and friends. She was careful who she admitted into her heart, but once you were there, she would never let you down. Grace was strong. She was a silent leader at an age when it is difficult to lead. Her friends learned from her example.

Grace loved her dog, Sugar. You could tell by the way she treated and talked about Sugar. Sugar brought her great joy. She loved and cared for that dog immensely.

I know Grace was an artist and a poet, but somehow, I always imagined she would be a doctor or a veterinarian when she grew up. She had the compassion for this kind of work. She had the smarts and dedication to get there. The only thing she did not have was enough time. She did not have the time to show us all what profession she would choose.

When we would get together with the Tam family, my husband would try to tease Grace: "How could she *really* be ten years old already? Why didn't she stay small? Could she make Steve's hair long like hers?" Grace was always one step ahead of him. She never fell for his silly teasing. She would look straight at him and make sure he knew she was taking none of that! Grace was a mature little girl who you could talk to like an adult. She was also fun to be with.

Grace will live with our family forever. She is a light that shines in our hearts. She gave us love and laughter whenever we were together. Today that love and laughter stays with us.

All our love
Heather, Steve, Matthew, and Amanda Margo
Friend

THE STINKY SHOES

Stinky shoes smell like poop
Which makes people go bu ho
They smell awful
Like rotten waffles
And make me look like
I am going to puke
I hate stinky shoes
And I will never wear
Stinky shoes

FERDINAND MAGELLAN

Magellan grew up in a queen's castle
Working and working for a messenger boy
His parents died when he was ten
But having a home is a joy
He stayed there for awhile
Magellan learned about explorers
He had a dream to be one
He traveled with his brother
To have an experience
One day I hope he would
Sailing! Sailing! To circle the world
To reach the Spice Islands
Five ships! Five Ships! Sailing
I wonder if he will return
Magellan died in the Philippines,
But I remember his dream

A Poem from Renee Navlet

I walked to the top of a mountain one day
In search of the natural beauty and
wonders of this earth abound
As I walked this path with
my loved ones around
I never anticipated that God's
plan for me that day
Would be so profound

The tragedy unfolded
family and strangers all around
Watched as the big snowball came down
We tried to help her with growing despair
This little girl who had flown in the air
Now lay before me on the ground
Life seemed so unfair

We worked while we waited
For help to arrive
Then we heard her
Take that last sigh

I watched as God held out his hand
And said come with me to the promised land
One life on earth ended
And a new one began
I sat there crying, chilled to the bone
As I watched while God guided
her to his heavenly throne

Our hearts were filled with great pain
As we began our descent back
down the mountain that night
I looked up to the heavens and
Imagined her surrounded by great white light
And heard her say, "I will see you again."
The heavens were rejoicing as
they welcomed her home
But those of us here on earth
Were left feeling so alone
Grace, sweet Grace, 6 months ago today.

Renee Ackerman Navlet
Monday, January 31, 2011
9:09 P.M.

JAPAN

I went to Japan.
There were lots to play,
lots to eat and,
my cousins were there.
We played like crazy,
all day long,
and had a bunch of fun,
all day long.
My relatives were there.
They took us to the fair,
and played with us there.
I had a lot of fun.
I wish I was there.
Although I know I will go there again,
I still was crying at my house.
I cried and cried for days and days,
but I know I will go there again.

A Letter from Cousin Hikaru

When the sad news was delivered, I thought it was a bad joke. Remember, Grace last time you were here, no one told me you were coming and you surprised me a lot. But I found out it was true, I was so sad. I wished it was a joke.

I have countless fun memories with Grace, playing seek and hide so intensively inside the house, having a blast with DS game match... I can't tell them all.

You sent me emails many times asking to come over to your place. I am sorry that I postponed visiting you so long, saying that I am too busy with school and sports. I regret I didn't respond your mail sooner and even when I did, my response didn't sound sincere.

Grace, I know you are worried so much, I can imagine you are still worrying about your family and relatives. Don't worry, Grace. Everything is all right here.

I promise you I never forget you. I promise I never give up my life no matter how much pain and sadness I need to go through. Because I have decided to live and enjoy the life for you, and because I know you would love to live much, much longer. I promise you I am going to be a good big brother for William. Don't worry. Please rest in peace and watch over us.

Thank you, Grace, for being with me like a younger sister, giving me fun memories, showing sweet affection, and encouraging my lazy self.

See you sometime.

Cousin Hikaru

TRAVELING

Pack! Pack! Pack your bags
1, 2, 3! Suitcases
Make sure you have clothes
Check! Check! Check!
Ready here we go!
In the airplane can be boring
But soaring in the air can be fun
I like to eat snacks
In the airplane can be noisy
But sleeping is relaxing
In your hotel is very relaxing
You can sleep and eat
Not noisy and very cozy
You can watch TV and go out to places
I think hotels are the best part about traveling

A Letter from the
Lawler Family

When John and Tamami asked us to write something about Grace, my husband Dave and I were deeply honored. As we thought about what we wanted to say though, the words proved to be more difficult to find than we expected. Casting a spotlight onto Grace feels awkward, because she was never the type of girl that would seek out attention for herself. Because of that, her gentle presence felt more like a warm summer breeze than a heavy gust of wind, yet the impression she left will be with us forever.

When we first met Grace, she was the adorable, chubby-cheeked preschooler who lived next door, full of all of the energy you'd expect from a little girl who was about to turn five. The first time that Grace joined us for dinner, we sat around the table, folded our hands, and then I asked our daughter Jamie and her younger sister Kristen to say "grace." Grace instantly sat up, wide-eyed, as if she'd done something wrong; Dave and I laughed, and then rephrased our request for "the dinner prayer." Even in her modesty, Grace had a way of making people smile. Over these last six and half years, from tea parties and games of Duck Duck Goose to Hannah Montana karaoke, dressing up as Charlie's Angels, and sunny afternoons in the pool, we have watched her grow into a beautiful young lady, with all of the elegance that her name embodies.

Grace was such a wonderful influence on Jamie. She truly was the type of friend that you wish for your children—kind, intelligent, self-motivated, humble, compassionate. When Jamie was with Grace, we never had to worry about where they were or what they were doing; Grace always set a good example for making the right choices. Consequently, on days when my husband and I had studying to do or work to catch up on, we'd institute a "no visitors" policy for our daughters, but Grace was always the exception to the rule. She and Jamie would spend hours together, talking about all of the things that girls this age do: clothes, school, boys, pop stars, and everything in between. Even though Jamie was two years younger, Grace always treated her like an equal, and Jamie adored her for this. Jamie understood that Grace had close friends in her own grade, but she still regarded Grace as her best friend. Every day, we miss seeing Grace's shy smile at our front door.

The two girls' personalities complemented each other well—Grace was the calm force, and Jamie was the entertainer. When Jamie would clown around, Grace would start to giggle, and in turn, Jamie would feed off of that and escalate her antics to the point where the two of them would be howling in fits of laughter. Of all of Grace's qualities, her laugh is the one that I miss the most. She had the cutest laugh.

Grace was terrific young lady, in large part because she had parents who made her and her brother William their priority. Whether it was a trip to Japan, a fun day at the Birch Bay waterslides, piano and Kung Fu lessons, or simply flying kites in the cul-de-sac, John and Tamami have worked hard to spend quality time with their children and give them a rich variety of experiences. I've never met a family that was so committed to each other, and their example makes us want to be better parents.

To that end, Dave and I took our girls for a family vacation at the end of July 2010. Our budget was tight, but we wanted to give our daughters some fun summer memories so we drove to

Seaside, Oregon. We spent a lot of time swimming in the hotel pool and making sandcastles at the beach, and periodically, we'd walk along Broadway Street to browse through the shops. Jamie was eager to find just the right souvenir for Grace, so she'd clutch her wallet full of Christmas money and patiently look through all of the displays, occasionally picking up items and saying, "Oh, Grace would love this." Eventually she settled on a palm tree necklace with a monkey-shaped case, and she bought a second one for herself so that they would have matching jewelry. After the long drive home on July 31, Jamie hopped out of the car and was excited to run next door to give Grace her treasure, but after seeing cars in the Tam's driveway, she came into the house and said, "I'd better not go now, Mom. They have company." That "company" turned out to be the search-and-rescue chaplain, who later came to our front door to break the news about Grace's accident, which had taken place only a few hours earlier.

In that moment, I was grateful that Jamie was playing in the yard with other friends and was out of earshot, for the grief was overwhelming. A swarm of thoughts raced through my head—Is this real? How can this happen? What can we do to help the Tams? And how are we going to tell

Jamie that her best friend is gone? We finally sat her down a few hours later for that very difficult conversation.

The day after Grace's passing, Jamie went with me to visit John, Tamami, and William. She brought the palm tree necklace and presented it to Tamami, explaining that she'd purchased two to serve as "friendship necklaces," and now she wanted Tamami to have Grace's. Tamami went into the kitchen and came back with a shirt and scarf set that Grace had picked out for Jamie's birthday, and she expressed that Grace had been very much looking forward to Jamie's slumber party, which was coming up in five days. It was surreal watching the two of them exchange gifts on Grace's behalf, as if Grace was simply away for the afternoon.

In many ways, though, we've learned that Grace is still here. Although her spirit is in heaven, parts of her remain to serve as indelible reminders of her life and the mark that she left on this world. In her name, changes are on the way to the Verlot ice caves so that a tragedy like this can't happen to another family. All around her community, parents are reevaluating their priorities. At her elementary school, a tree is being planted as a symbol of her young life and the light she brought to the people she touched. In her neighborhood, a memorial bench is being installed at the pond where she walked her beloved dog, Sugar, so that her parents, brother, and friends have a place to sit and reflect. And here in our house, Jamie has a special box where she has stowed away keepsakes and reminders of her friend, so that during those frequent times that she's missing Grace, she has a place to go to find some peace.

We miss you, Grace. Thank you for blessing Jamie with your friendship. When we feel that warm breeze, we'll be thinking of you.

Love,

Lauri, Dave, Jamie, and Kristen Lawler

Neighbor

♡ LOVE IS ... ♡

Love is like an end of a rainbow,
that covers your heart with lots of red roses.
It makes your face smile,
with blushes of hearts and
makes you happy all day long.
Love is loving a family
and a child of your own.
You can say I love you,
but you need to show it all.
Love is just like,
happiness and joy.
Love is a feeling of a human being.
Love is a person who cares for you
and shows they love you with all their heart.
You can only love a certain person
and loving a person showing you care.
Love is like an animal caring,
and making a smile while hugging.
And that is what love explains to me.
(On the occasion when one of her teachers
getting married.)

A Letter from Dad

As a father, I always think *do I love my children enough, do I show them that I love them?* The question / answer is an unending puzzle for me.

Since the horrible accident half of my soul has been frozen. No matter what I am doing, thought of Grace never fades from my mind. I will forever struggle how to spend the rest of my life without Grace's presence. One of bereaved parent wrote that she had a life before and has a life after. I am feeling the same way. There is no good or bad, no superior or inferior, but just the life has become different.

Grace was very special to me. Since my job as a contract Engineer brought me to Germany, France, Dallas TX, and Pittsburgh PA, she followed me everywhere with her mother. Just seeing her smile after a long work day made me so happy and proud. Her first word was *pool*. She said, "Pool" when she pointed out the pump up swimming pool in our backyard. If I remember correctly her second word was *Dada*. The sweet sound of Dada thrilled me and I often boasted she said dada first before mama.

Before being a parent, I had decided to be a dedicated father and help my children to experience their life. Both Grace and her younger brother William were very shy but I could tell both of them had tremendous enthusiasm to interact with the outside world. Touching sands on the beaches, chasing baby crabs, flying a kite on a storming windy day, travel to the different counties and immense in the different culture, visiting animal shelters, and participating in fund raiser for good cause.

I tried to teach them, but it was them who taught me. Especially Grace was an embody of virtues like fairness, responsibility, respect, and compassion.

My memories of Grace is vast, full of joy even on the last day of her passing during the hike up she would share half of a wild huckleberry with me. Grace was a very caring and sharing person. She would always give in when we ask for opinion to make a decision for family outing or activity, she taught me how to be a father rather than me teaching her. Grace cared for anyone no matter whether she knew them or not. She spent her time collecting for charity and donate to charity.

Yet Grace never take life for granted. She believe in giving much more than taking.

Grace often reach out to make new friends wherever she goes. Her actions tells me she face any challenge, overcome any sorrow, unfold life's mystery then struggle and fight solving the puzzle to accomplish life's journey, her actions has always been to fulfill any promise not only to satisfy herself but more so to please others.

I recalled one night asking Grace when she was three to stop wetting her diaper, she told me she will stop and next morning she was dry and almost always she was dry after that.

This is close to the end, I would like to convey my thought.

In life it is not how much we spend our time with our children, rather it is how *quality* time we spend. It's too late to say I would like to do things differently, but we try our best to spend quality time with them. Now the time ended with Grace, and we must realize and remember her as she was and all the *quality* time we have had will never end. I just wish we had more *quality* time coming than just eleven years; that is too *short*.

Dad